SEEING THE
BIG
PICTURE

of the Bible

KING'S
WORD
PUBLISHERS

All proceeds from the sale of this book go to support the ministry of Kingswood University.

Seeing the Big Picture of the Bible:

Reading the Bible as God's Story of Reconciliation

STEPHEN J. LENNOX, PH.D.

Dedication

To my wife, Eileen, my dearest friend.

Table of Contents

Acknowledgments

I can't possibly thank all the people who have been instrumental in the preparation of this book since it represents the accumulation of the past 40 years of formal biblical study.

There are several people who have provided me with significant help along the way. I'm grateful to Dr. Laurence Mullen of Houghton College who provided my first formal introduction to the Bible and to the late Dr. David Dorsey who inspired me to find God's character and plan in Scripture. Former colleagues, Dr. Ken Schenck, Dr. Chris Bounds, and Dr. Keith Drury were so helpful in refining these views. I owe special thanks to Keith. Although we are no longer faculty colleagues, he remains a dear friend who kindly and helpfully read this manuscript, offering many helpful insights.

I value the time I was able to spend writing in the tranquility of the Pocono mountains, courtesy of my brother-in-law and sister-in-law. Thank you, Barry and Audrey.

I am especially grateful to the students and colleagues at Kingswood University, and to the many laity who have enriched this material with their questions and insights.

Introduction

I love forests. I love the great stands of trees that surround me where I live. Not just a few, but thousands of maples, birches and all kinds of evergreens carpet the hills for miles on end.

I also love walking among the trees, hiking the many beautiful trails in this region. But there's a problem. When walking in the woods, I can easily "miss the forest for the trees." I can see the trees but not how they all fit together into a forest. If I'm not careful, I can become lost in the forest among the trees.

It helps to get the big picture. I get the big picture when I fly over the area where I live and can see the lay of the land. I also get the big picture through a map, which shows how all the parts fit together. This lets me appreciate the "trees" even more and helps me avoid getting lost.

"Missing the forest for the trees." We use this expression to describe getting so close to something we lose our perspective. We can see the individual parts but not how they fit into the whole. It's like studying the individual pieces of a mosaic or jigsaw puzzle without any sense of how they all fit together to form a picture.

This can happen when reading the Bible. We read one of the Bible's stories, like the one about David fighting Goliath, but aren't sure how that story fits with other stories. What does David have to do with Moses or Paul or me? If we lose sight of the forest—the big story—and see only the trees—the individual stories or details within those stories—we can end up reading the Bible like an anthology, a collection of loosely connected tales.

Complicating matters is the size of this book, more than a thousand pages in most versions. Nor is everything in this big book a story. We also find lists of names, poems, proverbs, laws, visions, pronouncements and more. How do all these fit together in the big picture?

And what do all these parts have to do with Jesus? We know He is a major character in the Bible, but He doesn't appear until more than halfway through. Should we look for Him in the Old Testament? If so, where? If not, do we even need to pay attention to the Old Testament?

To make matters worse, when we enter the Bible's pages, we find ourselves in a different world. As Dorothy observed when arriving in Oz, "we're not in Kansas anymore." We meet people with strange names from unfamiliar places doing things we didn't think people should do and talking about things we're not acquainted with.

Tools like a study Bible and a Bible dictionary can help explain some of these mysteries, but even then, it can feel like we're missing the point. Such tools help us see the trees more clearly, but they don't necessarily help us see the forest. We need to see the big picture of the Bible.

That is what I want to provide in this book. I want to take us up to an altitude where the Bible's overarching story becomes visible. I want this book to be like a map that guides you through the various parts of the Bible, showing how they all fit together to tell the big story. I hope reading the chapters that follow will be like studying the cover of the jigsaw puzzle box: getting the big picture in mind so you can see how the pieces come together.

Briefly stated, the big story of the Bible is the story of God's desire to have a relationship with humanity. It begins with Him creating humanity to live harmoniously in four relationships: primarily with Him, but also with other people, with self, and with the created order. The Bible then tells how these relationships became damaged and how God set in motion a plan to restore them. The big story of the Bible is the story of reconciliation.

Jesus is the central figure in the plan of reconciliation. This isn't just what Christians claimed about Jesus, but what He claimed about Himself. Those in power didn't approve of His claims and killed Him. But that death and His subsequent return to life actually furthered God's plan. The rest of the New Testament describes how Jesus' life, death, and resurrection provides healing in all four broken relationships.

Learning from the Bible about God's plan to heal our broken relationships also reveals a lot about God. We'll learn how much He loves us and how powerful He is. We'll discover how much He reminds you of your kindergarten teacher but also of an African tribal chief and a bicyclist in Mozambique.

We'll watch how gradually God reveals Himself. For example, we see Him first as the One and Only God, what we call monotheism. These days, almost everyone thinks of God this way since most humans follow one of the three monotheistic religions: Judaism, Christianity, or Islam. But when God revealed Himself as singular, this was radical news. All the other cultures were polytheistic, believing in many gods.

Later in the Bible, God reveals that while He is essentially One, He expresses that singular essence in three persons. We call this the Trinity. Hints of this can be found throughout the Bible, but it becomes much clearer when God arrives in the person of Jesus and when Jesus sends the Spirit of God on the Day of Pentecost.

Our flight over the Bible will also teach us about God's "work-arounds." These are temporary measures, like the law of Moses, the family, and the Temple. God put them in place to help humans navigate life's difficulties until He completes His plan.

Paying attention to God's character and plan of reconciliation are two important helps in seeing the Bible's big picture. A third is understanding God's number one rule: You have to believe. "Without faith," writes the author of the Book of Hebrews, "it is impossible to please God" (Hebrews 11:6). So much of what God does and says in the Bible is intended to teach His followers to walk by faith.

You don't need to "miss the forest for the trees" when reading the Bible; you can see the big picture. Once you do, you'll gain a greater appreciation for the trees because you'll know how they fit together to form the forest. You'll be better able to appreciate the beauty of the stories and other types of literature in the Bible.

But knowing the big story will also allow you to walk among those trees without getting lost. The big clues like God's character, plan, and expectation will help you stay on the main trail and see what this book is all about.

We're calling this the Bible's big story for several reasons. For one, it is big, spanning a long time, involving lots of people who do lots of things. This story is an epic if there ever was one.

But the Bible's story is big for another reason: it is THE story. It tells the most important story you'll ever hear, the story that makes sense of all other stories. This story explains where everything came from and where it is going. It describes our true identity and what we're supposed to be doing. It explains how we can live the very best life possible. These are the questions everyone is asking, and the Bible provides the answers.

Once you know the Bible's big story you can understand and embrace the truth that allows you to live the life God intended. You can take your place in the biggest story of all, the story of God's love for you.

So, let me invite you to climb on board and buckle your seatbelt low and tight around your waist. We're about to take off for a flight over the forest we know as the Bible. Our first stop is the very first vista anyone ever had, the Garden of Eden.

Study Questions

1. According to the Introduction, what is the main point of the Bible?

2. What are the four main relationships?

3. What does the author mean by "work-arounds"?

4. What other work-arounds can you think of beside the three mentioned in the Introduction?

Chapter One
THE PERFECT BEGINNING
Genesis 1-2

The beginning of everything

Open the Bible and what do you see? Nothing but Someone. Then this Someone speaks and you begin to see everything. The God who has been there all along is responsible for everything else, using just His words.

For a long time, people have been discussing how quickly or slowly things appeared. Some Christians believe creation happened in six 24-hour periods; others believe it happened over billions of years.

Here is the one point on which all Christians can firmly agree: whatever is, is because of God. As the Apostles Creed puts it: "I believe in God the Father Almighty, maker of heaven and earth."

I find it helpful to think of the opening two chapters of Genesis as a counter-argument. The creation account we find there was actually written to challenge other ancient versions of how things came to be.

The Israelites were likely well-acquainted with these other creation accounts, such as the ones believed by the ancient Egyptians and Mesopotamians (present day Iran and Iraq). The Genesis account was written to contradict and replace these other versions in the minds of God's people.

By the time Genesis was written (around 1200-1400 BC), the Israelites had already spent several centuries living in the land of Egypt. They knew the Egyptian creation accounts well. They knew the story of how a single god created all the other gods and everything else from bodily fluids like saliva and semen and through various physical actions. Another Egyptian version described a god who brought everything into existence by speaking. Egyptians understood creation to involve the emergence of solid ground out of water, order out of chaos.

The Israelites would also have known the Mesopotamian creation accounts. In one such account, Enuma Elish, a single god created other gods who then began to fight with one another. After this celestial battle, the victorious gods created humanity as an afterthought, to be their servants. They took the blood of one of the defeated gods and mixed it with clay to form humans.

Since the Genesis account was written to counter these other accounts, it's helpful to compare and contrast them. First and foremost, in the biblical account God rules alone. The other stories picture a chief god, but always as one among many. The Genesis creation story is unique among other ancient Near East accounts for its emphasis on a single, all-powerful God who works His will with His creation.

Second, these other accounts describe the gods as part of the creation. Outside of Israel, people worshiped the sun, moon, earth, sky and other parts of nature because they considered them divine. The biblical account makes a sharp distinction between the single God who created everything and everything He created. He is divine and it is not.

This is very clear when you read the biblical account of the creation of the sun, moon, sky, stars and the rest of the natural world. It is even more clear later when God expressly forbids His people from worshiping anything in the natural world (see Exodus 20:4-5).

Making a sharp distinction between God and His creation also explains a phrase repeated several times in Genesis 1. We're told that God created things to reproduce "according to their kind" (see verses 11, 12, 21, 24 and 25). The author of Genesis makes clear that God designed nature to be self-perpetuating. So, fruit trees grow from seeds according to the laws by which God designed nature to operate.

In the other creation accounts, nature is not self-perpetuating, but requires continuous divine involvement. If people wanted crops to grow, they must persuade the gods responsible for the soil and rain through some form of sacrifice.

In the biblical account, God separated Himself from nature. Of course, He can intervene to send the rain or stop it, to help the crops grow or prevent their growing. But God designed nature to operate on its own, according to the observable laws of nature.

This, by the way, is why humans can practice science. If nature did not operate by observable laws, we couldn't study nature and learn how to cooperate with it. Any talk of a conflict between the Bible and science misses this point. The opening chapters of Genesis contain an invitation to scientific study.

A third difference between the biblical creation account and all others is how God created everything out of nothing (sometimes referred to by the Latin phrase, *creatio ex nihilo*). In the other creation accounts, matter—the stuff from which things are made—already existed. The gods used this matter to create everything else.

In the biblical account, there was nothing to work with until God spoke. The writer of the Book of Hebrews puts it this way, "By faith we understand that the universe was formed at God's command, so that what is seen was not made out of what was visible" (Hebrews 11:3). In the beginning, there was nothing but a Someone.

Viewed against the ancient Near East background, we see a fourth emphasis in the biblical account, one involving the question of whether humans were created essentially evil, or whether they were created essentially good but then became evil.

Israel agreed with its neighbors that humans were sinful; that reality is hard to ignore. The question is, were we created this way or did we become this way? According to the Mesopotamian account, we were created this way. Humans were made from the blood of an evil god so evil comes naturally to us. We can't help ourselves when we sin, because we are essentially sinners.

The biblical picture is very different. Genesis 1 and 2 make it very clear that humans were not created sinful. That corruption occurs later, as described in Genesis 3. In other words, sin is alien to humanity, like a virus in the human body. Evil grows in the garden of the human heart, but as a foreign weed, not a native plant.

According to God, to commit sin is to behave in a subhuman and unnatural way. Sinful behavior is completely out of character for a human being. To rid the heart of sin would make us more human, not less.

Still another difference between the creation accounts is the emphasis placed on humanity. According to the Mesopotamians, humans were an afterthought, created as slaves so the gods wouldn't need to carry their own wood and draw their own water.

The Bible agrees that humans were made to serve God, but our service is very different. According to Genesis, we aren't slaves, but stewards. We were created to manage the Master's estate.

This helps explain a sixth way the Genesis creation account differs from those of Israel's neighbors. In those stories, humans are an afterthought. In Genesis, humans are God's masterpiece, the culminating moment of the creation extravaganza, the grand finale, like on Independence Day when fireworks light up the sky. Over and over God had looked at His day's labors and pronounced the results good (see Genesis 1:4, 10, 12, 18, 21, 25). But when Adam and Eve show up, things go from good to "very good" (Genesis 1:31).

Most impressive of all, a comparison between the biblical creation account and those of Israel's ancient neighbors emphasizes that humans were actually made in God's image (see Genesis 1:26-28). In other cultures, humans made gods in their image; in the Bible, God makes humans in His image.

Made in God's image

That each of us is made in God's image is a game-changer. This identity trumps all other identities. More important than anything else about me, my gender, race, socio-economic status, abilities, disabilities, appearance, intelligence, or experience, being made in God's image is the most important thing about me.

This reality changes how I look at myself. Whether I take pride in some aspect of my identity, like my social status or education, or whether I demean myself because of something I see inside, I am making the same mistake. I am focusing on something of lesser importance and ignoring what matters most, something for which I can take no credit, something that makes us all equal in God's eyes.

To be made in God's image changes how we look at others. Social class, education, lifestyle, appearance, race, intelligence—society tends to categorize people this way, and ranks us accordingly. That every human is made in God's image means that the most important thing about us is shared by all of us. Valuing people by any other standard makes no sense.

More specifically, being made in God's image includes what some call the natural image. Many of our attributes, like creativity, reason, an appreciation for beauty, and a sense of justice, are also possessed by God, although He has them to a perfect extent. So, when we create something beautiful, we are displaying a god-like quality, manifesting the natural image of God. So too when we advocate for justice or think deep thoughts, we're taking after our heavenly Father. This is true, by the way, whether someone believes in God or not.

To be made in God's image also means we serve as God's representatives on earth. This is often referred to as the political image of God. After creating humans, God gave them a job: to rule over the earth and subdue it (Genesis 1:26, 28).

To rule over and subdue sounds violent and destructive, but God intended quite the opposite. He wanted us to become so attentive to and familiar with what He created that we became proficient in bringing out the best that nature has to offer.

A third aspect involved in the image of God is what is sometimes called the corporate image. When God announced His intention to create people, He said, "Let us make mankind in our image" (Genesis 1:26). Do you notice the plurals: "us" and "our?" Many see God hinting here at the fact that He exists as three persons, what we call the Trinity.

God seems to be suggesting that He is not only One (monotheism), He is also more than one. Jesus will make this clearer when He comes. Although a faithful Jew (that is, holding firmly to monotheism), Jesus claims to be equal with God. After His ascension, Jesus will send the Holy Spirit on Pentecost, which helps us understand that the Spirit is also God.

The Trinity may be Christianity's most puzzling belief. For God to be three yet one seems like a mathematical impossibility. But the Trinity is not illogical, it's just multi-dimensional. It's like shifting your thinking from a square to a cube. With a square you think in two dimensions: length and width, but with a cube you add the dimensions of height and depth.

God is one in one way and three in another. He is singular in His essence but expresses that singularity in three persons. For example, you are singular in your essence—there's only one of you—but you express that essence in many ways, such as parent, child, sibling. One, yet more than one.

Perhaps a better example might be the human race. We think of humanity as a single essence, but we understand that singular essence as composed of multiple humans. One, yet more than one.

I know it's complicated. Perhaps this is one reason why God took so long to reveal it. Then too, revealing His nature gradually fits well with His intention that we live by faith.

But what does any of this have to do with being made in God's image? When God speaks of Himself in Genesis 1:26 in the plural, "let *us* make . . . in *our* image," He is not only referring to His nature as Three in One. He is also making it clear that to be made in His image is to be made for relationship. Just as the three persons in the Trinity exist in perfect harmony with each other, always getting along, so humans were created for relationship with other humans.

Perhaps the most important aspect of being made in the image of God is our capacity to be in a relationship with Him, sometimes called the moral image. The moral image was what enabled the first humans to be comfortable in God's presence. Adam could talk with God because he was, so to speak, tuned to the frequency on which God was broadcasting. You might say he spoke God's language. Adam not only heard God, he was able to do what God commanded. Even better, Adam wanted to do God's will.

These are the standard ways of speaking about the image of God, but they aren't the only ways. We can also describe what it means to be made in the image of God by thinking about four relationships.

Another way of thinking about the Image of God

Each human was created for four relationships: to be in relationship with God, in relationship with other humans, in relationship with himself or herself, and in relationship with the natural world. We can see these four relationships at play in the opening two chapters of Genesis.

Human to God

When the first humans were created, they enjoyed a perfect relationship with God. The moral image was fully operational, allowing unhindered communication and willing obedience. This is what we find in Genesis 1:28-30. God instructed them to

> "Be fruitful and increase in number; fill the earth and subdue it. Rule over the fish in the sea and the birds in the sky and over every living creature that moves on the ground." Then God said, "I give you every seed-bearing plant on the face of the whole earth and every tree that has fruit with seed in it. They will be yours for food." . . . And it was so.

God commanded and humans obeyed.

Adam and God work well together, as we see in Genesis 2:19, where God brought the animals and Adam named them. They can even co-produce another human, as in Genesis 2:20-23, the end result being Eve. You get the impression that the relationship between God and the first humans is harmonious.

It also has great potential for good, both for the first couple, and through them to the world and all those who will follow and fill it. Living in harmony with God will allow them to experience the best of what this new world has to offer. By carrying out God's will according to God's design, the earth would be orderly, occupied, and understood.

Human to human

A second relationship each human was created to enjoy was inter-personal, human to human. We were made to get along well with others. We see that this was part of God's intention in Genesis 2:20-24, the first wedding. After determining "it is not good for the man to be alone" (Genesis 2:18), God set about to fix the problem.

The first step was to demonstrate to Adam that a "helper suitable for him" (Genesis 2:18) did not already exist; Adam couldn't find one anywhere among the animals. This is the reason for the parade of animals in verse 19. Adam met each animal and named it. In other words, he didn't just see the animal, he knew it well enough to know what to call it. When the parade came to an end, Adam had seen all the animals and come to know them well, but "for Adam no suitable helper was found" (Genesis 2:20b).

To solve Adam's problem, God would have to create someone new, which He did through the first surgical operation. Adam is anesthetized, a rib extracted, the wound closed, the rest of Eve created and attached to the rib, and Eve is brought into existence. When she is brought to Adam, he reacts with delight. "This is it," he realizes, the one he has been looking for, someone made just for him (see Genesis 2:23).

The human to human relationship is most fully expressed in marriage, but can be experienced in other ways, such as true friendships. God created each human to be part of a community; this is the only way to become fully human. As expressed by John Donne, 17th century clergyman and poet, "No man is an island."

Human to self

Each human is also created to have a healthy relationship with himself or herself, intra-personal harmony. Such harmony allows you to see yourself clearly, as you really are. You interact with others in ways that are mutually beneficial. Rather than loving others for your own sake or loving others instead of yourself, you love others as you love yourself. In this kind of healthy relationship, you are able to open yourself to God, free of fear, free of guilt, and free of shame. You are content.

Our culture is much more attuned to this intra-personal relationship than earlier cultures. Ancients didn't define the "self" quite the way we do. They were much more attentive to how each person fit together with other selves. Even so, when we look at Genesis 1-2, we see Adam at peace with himself and Eve with herself.

God instructs them to rule over the earth and subdue it. How would you respond to such a command? I could instantly come up with a dozen reasons why that wouldn't be possible and why He should choose someone else. How do Adam and Eve respond? We aren't told explicitly, but they seem to take up the challenge right away. That could only happen if they were at peace within themselves, free of the fear that keeps us from obeying God's commands, free of the shame that believes the lies we tell ourselves.

God lays down certain rules about what they are to eat and not eat (see Genesis 1:29; 2:16-17). At least for a season, Adam and Eve obeyed. This wouldn't have happened unless they were at peace with themselves. Otherwise they would have responded with pride ("I know what is best") or fear ("How do I know God's command is best for me") or shame ("What will Eve think if she sees me eating this?").

The clearest picture in these chapters of intra-personal harmony is found in the closing verse of Genesis 2: "Adam and his wife were both naked, and they felt no shame" (25). Imagine that, completely exposed before God and each other, yet unashamed.

Human to nature

The fourth relationship for which humans were created is with the world in which we live. In other words, humans were made to be at home in God's creation. We were made with the capacity to discover the secrets of the universe and to learn how to employ those secrets for the good of the world and its inhabitants.

That this is our calling as humans is implied in God's command to the first couple to "subdue" the earth (Genesis 1:28). Subdue doesn't mean dominate and destroy, although we have all-too-often taken this approach to the natural world.

To subdue means to master, to become experts at making the most of the world in which we live. When you master a skill, like playing the violin or learning a language, the end result looks effortless and sounds beautiful. The mastery is so complete, people assume you were born with that skill.

In a healthy relationship between humanity and this world, work is not a bad thing. Work, for many, is a necessary evil, required to pay the bills. But God designed something better. He intended each of us to participate with Him in His work by doing our work. Blessed is the person who understands how their job allows them to partner with God while getting paid for it! Blessed is the person who lives with a sense of calling.

When this relationship is as it should be, work becomes an adventure of discovering the laws by which the world works, and how to make the most of those laws. Work allows us to become experts at what we do for our good, the good of others, the good of the world, and the glory of God.

We see this healthy human to nature relationship in Adam's ability to name the animals. He perceives the essence of the animal and describe it in a name. Naming implies mastery; Adam was created to be master of his domain.

Made for harmony

To be made in the image of God is to be created to experience full harmony in these relationships. The most important of the four is human to God. If this one is sound, it creates the possibility for the others to be as well. If this relationship is unsound, none of the others can be right.

These four relationships were not just for Adam and Eve. Every one of us is made in God's image, therefore every one of us is made to experience harmony with God, with others, with ourselves, and with the universe. This remains as true today as ever.

The Bible opens with the story of how everything began. By Himself, out of nothing, without a struggle, God created the universe. He made everything as a home for his masterpiece, humanity. When Adam and Eve were in place, everything was "very good."

Humans were made in God's image. They shared a strong family resemblance with their Creator. They took up their responsibility to work alongside Him in this world. They shared His capacity to live in harmony with each other. Most importantly, they were made for a relationship with Him.

From this relationship with God flowed all the other relationships. They lived in harmony with each other, they lived at peace within themselves, and they were at home in the Garden.

Clearly, we aren't living in the Garden anymore. Alienation, not harmony is the norm. We are estranged from God. We cannot seem to get along with each other. We are out of touch with ourselves, more likely to live with shame than without it. We don't feel at home in the world. Work has become something we do just to pay the bills; we can't wait for the weekend and the endless weekend known as retirement. And yet we still hunger for harmony in these relationships.

Humans retain remarkable qualities like creativity, reason, and justice, but we use these to glorify ourselves and harm others, hardly God's original design. How did we get from the Garden to this? This is where the Bible takes us next.

Study Questions

1. The biblical creation account was written to counter rival accounts found among Israel's neighbors. We mentioned seven differences between those accounts and the biblical account. Which of these seven stood out to you the most and why?

2. What do we mean when we talk about the natural, political, corporate and moral image of God?

3. When you think of yourself as made in God's image, what stands out as most significant?

4. What are the four relationships each human is meant to possess? Describe the essence of each in your own words.

Chapter Two

SPOILED

Genesis 3

The fall

Decisions are the hinges upon which life's door swings. God created humanity to experience harmony in every way that mattered, but a series of decisions turned that harmony to pain.

Genesis 3 opens with reference to a crafty serpent. In the ancient Near East, snakes were feared, not just for their venom, but for their connection with matters of life and death. Perhaps it has something to do with the snake's ability to shed its skin. Israel and many of her neighbors used the snake to represent powerful forces.

Later Jews and Christians, with the benefit of hindsight, recognized that the serpent was not acting alone but under the influence of Satan, the enemy of our souls. In other words, what we witness in the actions of this snake in the garden is Satan using the natural world to tempt humanity to make poor decisions; it won't be the last time our Enemy employs this tactic.

The serpent began with a question designed to confuse Eve. "Did God really say, 'You must not eat from any tree in the garden'?" (Genesis 3:1). Notice how he twisted God's prohibition against eating from the tree of the knowledge of good and evil (Genesis 2:16-17) to suggest that God had prohibited eating any fruit from any tree in the garden.

Eve tried to clarify God's command, but we can see that Satan's strategy of confusion is already working. She fails to mention which tree was prohibited and adds something to God's command, a prohibition against even touching the fruit.

Having sowed confusion regarding God's command, the serpent turned next to challenge God's character as truthful and generous. Although God had clearly said that eating the fruit would lead to death, the serpent countered that such a punishment would never happen. Instead, humans would actually gain what they currently lacked: their eyes would be open, they would become like God, and they would gain knowledge, specifically the knowledge of good and evil (see Genesis 3:5).

Eve's fateful decision to eat the fruit may have resulted in part from confusion regarding God's command and God's character, but there were other factors, some of them of God's own doing. Eve noticed the fruit of the tree was appetizing ("good for food") and attractive to look at ("pleasing to the eye") (Genesis 3:6). Humans were created with an appetite so they would be sure to satisfy the body's need for energy. They were also created with an appreciation for beauty; this is part of being made in God's image.

Eve took the fruit and gave it to her husband, something that would have been less likely if God had not united the two into one flesh through marriage. Even the ability to make this terrible choice was possible because they were made in God's image. The Enemy turned God's gifts against Him.

I'm not suggesting that God should be blamed for their bad choices. It's just that sin is always about turning God's good gifts against Him. Eve's appetite, appreciation for beauty and relationship with Adam are precious things. Used in the proper way, they bring happiness. Turned against God and for the wrong purposes, they bring heartache.

Behind the confusion regarding God's word and character and the corruption of His good gifts, the first sin resulted from pride and fear. We see pride most clearly in humanity's desire to be like

God. We also see it in their failure to prioritize God's command, in their assumption that they deserved more than what God had determined was best for them, and in their presumption that they knew more than God.

With sufficient faith in God, they would have recognized He would never withhold from them anything good. They would have understood that God's blessings follow obedience. Adam and Eve were afraid they were missing out; the presence of fear always drives out faith.

The consequences of the fall

Alienation from God

The sin of the first couple created monstrous consequences. Before it they enjoyed fellowship with God and freedom in His presence. Now when they heard Him coming, they hid. Whereas earlier God had been able to provide words of direction and promises of blessing, now they hear correction and the promise of pain.

The problem is not that God is unwilling to forgive. He does forgive. He even shows compassion for their needs by giving them a new wardrobe so they won't feel such shame. Even before they asked, He provided a way to cope with the consequences of sin.

Humanity has discovered the very painful truth that while God forgives, sin always has consequences. These consequences spread to others within our network of relationships. When you are the first humans, from whom all other humans will come, those relationships include everyone. We all suffer because of their sin.

God addresses the serpent as part of the natural world (as we'll see below), but also as the manifestation of Satan. In the reference to Eve's son crushing the serpent's head and the serpent biting his heel (see Genesis 3:15), we glimpse the desperate battle for the human soul, with God seeking our best and Satan seeking our destruction. It will take centuries for God's people to understand the nature and magnitude of this battle, but when they do they point back to this verse as the first prediction of God's victory through the woman's offspring.

By the time this chapter ends, Adam and Eve are forced to leave the Garden. They must go, not because of God's anger, but because of His love. Because of their sin they had broken their relationship with God and could do nothing to repair it. God knows, if they remain, they might eat from the tree of life and live forever, making their alienation permanent (see Genesis 3:22-23).

Alienation from each other

The close relationship that Adam and Eve had with each other was also broken. They remained together, but lost the intimacy they once knew. Adam had responded to Eve's creation with "this is it"; now he points the finger of blame: she made me do it (see Genesis 3:12). Created as partners, now Eve is told that Adam "will rule over" her (Genesis 3:16).

Even in a "fallen" world, marriage remains God's plan for men and women. The home created by marriage is the best way to shape a community and culture. Research supports experience that marriage is a good way to grow up and develop one's character. Marriage is the best environment in which to bring up children with the proper values, children who will then go on to influence culture.

God designed marriage for good, but the brokenness that marks human-to-human relationship prevents the full realization of what God intended for marriage. The same could be said for every other relationship. We only have to turn to Genesis 4 before we see the first premeditated murder, and that by one brother against another.

Alienation from self

With their disobedience, Adam and Eve lost the intra-personal harmony they had known. Whereas before they had been naked and unashamed, now they see their nakedness and try to cover it up with fig leaves (Genesis 3:7). They were no more naked than before, but now they felt shame.

When they heard God, they hid in fear. At God's confrontation, they accused others rather than taking responsibility for their actions (see Genesis 3:12-13). We never hear them apologize. Fear, blame, self-defensiveness . . . these are the marks of intra-personal alienation.

Alienation from nature

Their sin also fractured their relationship with the natural world. The serpent was (much later) understood to represent Satan. Earlier his role in this story was as a part of nature that stepped out of its appointed place and was now cursed. Before this humans and animals appear to have been on favorable terms, now the serpent would be at odds with humanity. It would inflict pain on humans by biting their heels, but humans would inflict the greater pain when stepping on the snake's head.

The woman would also know physical pain, specifically the agonizing pain of labor and childbirth. And she would know the emotional pain of having lost her place of equality beside her husband.

Pain would come to the man as well, for he would have to struggle with the soil for food. All of nature is now at odds with humanity. How ironic! Schooled by the divine Gardener (see Genesis 2:9, 15), Adam must now struggle to gain his living by painful toil, fighting for food from the fields against thorns and thistles (see Genesis 3:17-18). Created to master the universe, Adam is now a slave to the soil.

"Coming of age"

Throughout the centuries, the "fall" has been seen as a disaster, creating problems with which all humans must reckon. More recently, many have seen something positive in these events, a maturation of humanity, a "coming of age." Adam and Eve encountered an obstacle—God's command—and made their own decision. They grew up.

The serpent tempted them with the knowledge of good and evil and they gained that knowledge, even if they paid a heavy price. To borrow a line from a popular song performed by singers from Sinatra to Elvis to Jay-Z: they did it their way.

For our culture, "coming of age" is a good thing, a necessary rite of passage. We mock the naïve "40-Year-Old Virgin" and celebrate the street-wise. We can relate to the themes in movies like "Dead Poet's Society" and "American Graffiti," TV shows like "Glee," and novels like *Catcher in the Rye*. We consider the transition from naïve childhood to mature adulthood worth it, even if it means pain and disillusionment. We consider knowledge of any kind worth any price necessary to obtain it.

Just to be clear, coming of age was God's idea first. He always intended humans to grow toward maturity. Even though Adam and Eve were created perfect, they were not created as finished products. God intended them to grow and mature in their perfection, developing in their relationships with Him, with each other, with self, and with creation.

The problem was not what they sought, but how they sought it. Satan convinced them God could only give them second best; if they wanted the best they would have to get it themselves. God wanted them to have the best but knew it would only be the best if they had it on His terms.

If you're a parent you want the best for your children, but you know the best depends on what they're able to handle. To give them something too soon could be disastrous; you'd never teach a toddler to drive. God knew the right conditions for them to experience the best, to come of age in the best possible way. Sin involves demanding the right things in the wrong way and at the wrong time.

Even after they disobeyed and reaped the disastrous results of their choices, God still planned to allow them to "come of age." We'll describe this plan in later chapters. For now, we can say that coming to share in the divine nature, gaining wisdom and knowledge, experiencing our full potential—God makes all these available to His children through salvation.

The continuing effects of the fall

The ripples begun in Genesis 3 continue today. That is why none of us are born in harmony with God; we are born with what some call "original sin." No one has to teach a toddler to be selfish, self-centered, demanding, ungrateful, aggressive, and deceitful. The prophet, Isaiah, wrote, "We all, like sheep, have gone astray; each of us has turned to our own way" (Isaiah 53:6). In the words of the apostle Paul, "all have sinned and fall short of the glory of God" (Romans 3:23).

Nor can we fix this problem on our own. We might feel bad about what we've done and try to do better, but even the most moral person living must confess they can't live up to God's expectations. Paul described us as being "dead" in our sins (Ephesians 2:1). He didn't mean we're physically dead, but that we are helpless to fix our problem. We're spiritually dead. When Adam and Eve sinned, they killed the moral image of God in themselves and in us.

Although the moral image of God was lost, the other aspects of the divine image remained. That might sound like good news, and in some ways, it is. But in other, very important ways, it isn't good news. Humans still have great qualities, but we tend not to use them as God intended. The very things that make humans remarkable allow us to become monsters.

We possess tremendous qualities, like reason and the ability to create, but now we turn them to our own purposes rather than employ them as intended, to glorify God and benefit others. History is filled with horrible examples of how we turned God's good gifts against Him, each other, ourselves, and the natural world. Think of the history of warfare in the modern period, the potential to destroy all of civilization through nuclear weapons, modern slavery, pornography, addictive drugs; the list goes on and on.

We were also created to live in harmony with each other and with ourselves. When sin enters the picture, the desire for this harmony remains but the capacity to satisfy this desire is gone. Now we hunger for intimacy but struggle to find it. When we do, we're constantly tempted to use the relationship for our own purposes, rather than in mutually beneficial ways.

When Adam and Eve sinned, they ruined everything for every one of us. We still have those god-like qualities and desires. We can still do good things and be nice people sometimes, but something has broken inside of us and we can't fix it.

"But," you might ask, "how did *their* sin affect *us*?" That is a good question. Some believe that as the first humans, Adam and Eve *represented* us. You and I have people who represent us in the halls of government, in courtrooms, in business offices. We don't always get to choose who those people are but we're stuck with the consequences of their choices.

Another explanation says that humans are a lot more *connected* than first appears. We tend to see ourselves as completely separate from others, what some call "buffered," like the coating on an aspirin. I make my decisions based on what I think is best and don't spend a lot of time considering the impact of my decision on others.

In fact, no one is really "buffered." Every choice we make has implications for others. Decisions made by one group of people impact others, even others in lands far away. My decision to purchase certain products in North America means that those who sell that product can continue to conduct business, whether in helpful or unhelpful ways.

If it is possible for us to be connected to others at a *geographical* distance, is it that much of a stretch that we might be connected to those who are *chronologically* distant? There are plenty of examples of how the effects of sin can linger through generations. One of my relatives made some very foolish decisions decades ago, the consequences of which continue to impact my life today.

This second theory makes even more sense in light of the science of genetics. Genes shape who we are and what we do but genes can be modified by behavior and passed along to future generations. Although it can't be proven, it isn't hard to imagine original sin being transmitted from Adam and Eve to all humans through our genes.

God surely must have known the disastrous consequences that would follow the sin of Adam and Eve. If so, why did He allow it? Why not nip all our problems in the bud?

He could have avoided creating in the first place, but He wanted humans to have the opportunity to enjoy fellowship with Himself. He could have created humans without the capacity to sin, but removing our freedom to choose would make us like robots. We would not only lack the capacity to sin, we would also lack the capacity to love.

God didn't want a race of robots. He made us in His image, which includes the freedom to choose. In the case of humans, the capacity to choose means the possibility of making the wrong choice. The God-given ability to reason means I can rationalize my bad decision and make myself feel justified.

As we saw earlier, God made us with physical desires like hunger, so that an appetizing piece of fruit creates a greater temptation. He made us with the capacity to appreciate beauty, so that an attractive piece of fruit is more tempting. God made us for relationships, so that the offer of a piece of fruit from our soulmate is hard to refuse.

God created humans with an appetite for more than food, for things like wisdom and spiritual maturity. This made it hard to resist the temptation to "become like gods, knowing good and evil" (Genesis 3:5).

There is another reason why God allowed the fall to happen. He knew, when all was said and done, humanity would be better off. There is an ancient Christian Easter hymn which refers to Adam and Eve's sin as a *felix* culpa, a "happy fault"; "O happy fault which deserved to have so great and glorious a Redeemer."

The early Christian teacher, St. Augustine, put it this way: "For God judged it better to bring good out of evil than not to permit any evil to exist." The same thought was expressed by the poet, John Milton, in these lines:

> O goodness infinite, Goodness immense!
> That all this good of evil shall produce,
> And evil turn to good; more wonderful
> Than that which creation first brought forth
> Light out of Darkness!

Because of this sin, said the Anglican preacher, John Wesley, humans are capable "of being more holy and happy on earth; and … of being more happy in heaven, than otherwise they could have been."

Without humanity's fall, Jesus would not have become human and we would never have seen what God looked like. We would never have seen the mysteries that make the angels curious (see 1 Peter

1:12). Unless humans had become sinful, wrote Wesley, "neither angels nor men could ever have known 'the unsearchable riches of Christ.'"

Even though we know God will redeem this tragedy, we cannot help but be grieved at the harm done through these wrong choices. We are grieved at the suffering that has resulted since those choices, suffering that continues today across the world, and that we know from personal experience.

We are also grieved when we realize how much we resemble Adam and Eve. Were we in their places, can we honestly say we would have chosen differently?

God has a plan and will begin to put this plan in place, but before then, we must see the serious and pervasive consequences of sin. Even those best suited to solve the problem prove powerless. No amount of human effort can undo these consequences. Warning: this next leg of our flight takes us over some pretty ugly territory.

Study Questions

1. Give real-life examples of the consequences of alienation in each of the four broken relationships:

    Human to God
    Human to human
    Human to self
    Human to the natural world

2. Why do you think "coming of age" is such an important cultural expectation?

3. How can we persuade people that God's plan for coming of age is better than the one offered by popular culture?

4. We've provided two possible explanations for how the sin of the first couple spread to all humans, either through representation or connection. Which explanation makes the most sense to you? Why? What other explanations might there be?

5. What do you think of the idea that the fall of humanity was, in fact, a "happy fault"?

Chapter Three

DEATH SPIRAL

Genesis 4-11

Cain and Abel

Genesis 4-11 are not easy reading. It's not just the difficult names and puzzling passages. It is having to watch the perfection God created in Genesis 1-2 come unraveled. Clearly, the choices made in Genesis 3 are producing a ripple effect that is turning very ugly, very quickly.

We have only just stepped into Genesis 4 before we witness the first murder, and that of one brother by another. Within this story we see what can happen when all four relationships experience alienation.

Human to human

The most obvious broken relationship is human to human, as Cain murders his own brother. What prompted him to do this was the alienation he felt within himself and, by implication, the alienation he felt from God.

That the boys had chosen different occupations was not a problem. Both farmer and rancher can carry out the creation mandate of "mastering" the earth. The farmer does so by understanding how to work with soil, seed, and weather to produce a harvest. The rancher must learn how to domesticate animals, care for them, help them multiply, and derive benefit from them.

That God preferred the fruit of Abel's labors over Cain's doesn't mean God likes ranchers more than farmers. We aren't told the reasons for God's choice, but we can speculate. Perhaps He wanted to emphasize the importance of costly sacrifice; Abel's offering required the animal to die.

Human to self

Cain's angry and dejected response to God's decision reveals intra-personal alienation. Cain misinterpreted God's choice as a criticism, a conclusion he would not likely have drawn had he been at peace with himself. The thoughts of a person already prone to shame naturally move in the direction of self-criticism.

God graciously makes clear to Cain that he is wrong to see this as a criticism (see Genesis 4:6-7), but Cain wasn't listening. Envy had taken over his heart. Jealous thoughts come to us all, but the emotionally-healthy person can acknowledge and set them aside. The person at odds with himself is more likely to become at odds with others, especially with those they perceive as rivals. "With only so much divine favor to go around," they reason, "I must get what I can, even if I have to take it from others." This envy festered in Cain's heart until he plotted, then committed the murder of his own brother.

Human to God

Cain's refusal to listen to God reveals alienation in this relationship as well. He didn't believe God's word of assurance, nor did he heed God's word of warning: "sin is crouching at your door; it desires to have you" (Genesis 4:7).

How sad that Cain refused to hear the hope God provided. After warning that sin waited outside with malicious intent, God assured Cain that he still had the power and responsibility to resist temptation: "you must rule over it" (Genesis 4:7). With

God's help, Cain could still say "no" to the murderous thoughts in his heart and "yes" to God's way.

Cain chose to ignore the voice of conscience, and it cost Abel his life. This inner voice of conscience continues to speak today. If we listen to it, we can make a better decision; we still possess enough of the divine image to do that. We can apply our reason and freedom of choice and refuse to do wrong.

Like our physical body, our conscience must get exercise in order to work properly. Even in tip-top shape, however, conscience is powerless to prevent sins that bypass our reason and will, nor will conscience solve our underlying sin problem. Though it cannot restore our broken relationship with God, conscience remains a work-around He provides to help us navigate in a fallen world.

Sin makes you stupid

Cain's choice reveals something else about sin: it makes you do stupid things. How would killing Abel solve Cain's problem? Would God not know what had happened? With Abel out of the way, would Cain become God's favorite? Would this murder convince God to like farm products more than animal sacrifice? Would killing Abel help Cain feel better about himself and make him happy again? It certainly wasn't fair to Abel. How would their parents feel when they learned that one of their sons was dead and the other his murderer?

The sinful heart can't think straight. Sin is like pain in that respect. When in pain it's very difficult to think clearly about anything else. Cain ignored God's warning, His offer of hope and every reasonable option and committed a senseless crime.

Even after the murder, his response to God displays no remorse, only deceit and self-justification (see Genesis 4:9). When we ignore the voice of conscience we not only become much more likely to commit senseless acts of sin, we also dull the edge of conscience, making us even more likely to sin still more.

We said earlier that all four fractured relationships are at play in this story. How is the human to nature relationship involved? The sin of Adam and Eve had made it more difficult to earn a living from the soil; Cain's sin drove him from the soil entirely. He would now become a "restless wanderer" (Genesis 4:12), doomed to wander the earth far from those he loved and the life he knew.

Only too late does Cain realize what he has done and appeal to God for help. Graciously, God provides ways for him to work around his new reality, alienated from God, from his family and friends, fearful for his life, and a stranger in a world he was supposed to manage.

The Bible makes it clear that sin is serious and spreading, but it also makes the point that human potential is not entirely lost. We saw that with the occupations chosen by Cain and Abel. We continue to find examples through the next several chapters.

We read, for example, about Cain marrying and establishing a city. Where, you ask, did Cain get his wife? I'd tell you if I were Abel. Seriously, we don't know for sure. God could have created a wife for Cain, but it seems more likely that Cain married his sister or another relative. The Bible doesn't provide every detail of these early days so it is possible that Adam and Eve had children about whom we've not been told.

It seems strange that after being told by God he would wander the earth, Cain builds a city. In the original it only says, "he built" (see Genesis 4:17), so we're left to wonder whether it was Cain or his son, Enoch, who actually built the city. In either case, we can see that Cain is trying to overcome the effects of his sin. God may have punished him with wandering, but he would still try to settle or at least he would encourage his son to settle.

The building of a city is a big accomplishment. So too are advances in animal husbandry, the invention of musical instruments, and the development of metalworking (see Genesis 4:20-22). We see in these verses people striving to recover their relationship with God, calling on the name of Yahweh, God's personal name (see Genesis 4:26). Even though fallen, humans continue to demonstrate that they are made in God's image. They possess gifts and seek a relationship with God.

Things get worse

They are also corrupted by sin, and corruption remains the dominant theme of these chapters. Lamech commits murder out of revenge for being injured, then boasts about it (see Genesis 4:23-24).

The opening verses of Genesis 6 reveal another serious example of corruption, although the nature of that offense remains a puzzle. The text tells us that the sons of God were marrying daughters of men. To know why that was wrong requires us to discover what is meant by "sons of God" and "daughters of men."

Some say the sons of God were angels who were marrying human women. This would explain why their offspring—part human, part angel—became "the heroes of old" (Genesis 6:4). This would represent a serious breach in God's plan, for He never intended angelic beings to marry, let alone marry humans. If this view is correct, it reveals that the rebellion we saw in the Garden is part of a larger and spreading rebellion against God.

A second possibility is that the sons of God were powerful individuals, like kings. We know these men sometimes used their power to force themselves on women. In ancient Mesopotamia there was something called the Rite of the First Night, when the king slept with a virgin on the night before she was to be married to someone else.

You see this referenced in the ancient piece of literature known as the *Epic of Gilgamesh*. One of the complaints about the king, Gilgamesh, was his insistence on sleeping with women prior to their wedding night. Even the *Epic of Gilgamesh* regards this treatment of commoners as oppressive. If this is the correct understanding, it illustrates an extreme example of human to human oppression.

Yet another possible explanation connects Genesis 6:1-4 with Genesis 4, which describes the descendants of the remaining sons of Adam and Eve: Cain (see Genesis 4:17-24) and Seth (see Genesis 4:25-5:32). We have already seen how Cain disobeyed God and how his offspring followed in his footsteps. Seth, on the other hand, is followed by righteous people, like Enoch (see Genesis 5:22-24) and Noah (see Genesis 5:28-32) who is later described as "a righteous man, blameless among the people of his time, and he walked with God" (Genesis 6:9).

This third view identifies the sons of God as the descendants of Seth, since they were generally more righteous, and the daughters of earth as those coming from the line of Cain. The problem, according to this view, was the intermarriage of righteous people with sinful, an arrangement that almost always weakens righteousness.

Which view is correct is hard to say, but they all share a common theme: the problem of sin was getting worse. In our discussion of Genesis 3 we noted that pain was the common result for everyone involved: for Adam in his labor, for Eve in childbirth, and for the serpent who would be crushed under the heel. Now we discover that even God is pained at how things have turned out. Genesis 6:6 says that Yahweh "was deeply troubled" at having made humanity; the verb here is the same one translated in Genesis 3 to describe the experience of pain. Sin has left everyone, even God, in pain with no hope in sight. Something needs to be done.

Noah, God's choice

What God did was choose Noah, a descendant of Seth. As we've noted, Noah had a reputation for righteousness surpassing that of his contemporaries. Noah's assignment was to build a boat, load it up with his immediate family and two of every kind of animal. God was going to destroy all other living creatures with a great flood. Only those on the boat would survive, and from these the world would be repopulated.

Others in the ancient world knew a similar story. As with the creation story, these versions provide a context against which to better understand the biblical account. One well-known flood story is found in the *Epic of Gilgamesh*. In both stories, a human is chosen to build a ship and load it with animals in order to weather a storm. Both ships land on a mountain and in both stories, the humans inside release a dove and a raven. Upon disembarking, both humans offer up a sacrifice.

There are also differences between the stories. Some are minor, like the size and design of the boat and the length of the storm. Others are more significant. For example, the gods in the Gilgamesh story gather like flies and dogs to smell the sacrifice, very un-godlike behavior. In the biblical story, when God smells Noah's burnt offering He makes a solemn promise to never again destroy the earth by flood.

In the Gilgamesh story, humans weren't supposed to know about the divine plan to flood the earth. The human was saved because someone leaked this knowledge to him. By contrast, Noah is sought out by God for his righteousness and informed of the divine plan.

Perhaps the most significant difference is the reason for the flood. In the Gilgamesh account, the gods were annoyed by human deficiencies, including how loud they were; the gods were having trouble sleeping. In the biblical story, humans were deficient, in fact, "the earth is filled with violence because of them" (Genesis 6:13). God's motive, however, was not personal inconvenience, but the restoration of His original plan for His glory and the good of humanity. Once again, such a comparison reveals the high value God places on people.

A vast flood took place in the ancient world. There is some question, however, whether it was global in scope, or over the then-known world, the Near East, or over a smaller region within this area. A straightforward reading of the biblical material suggests a global flood since the water covered "all the high mountains under the entire heavens" (Genesis 7:19) and destroyed "every living thing on the face of the earth" (Genesis 7:23). Certainly, God has the power to bring about such a flood on a global scale.

Among the problems with this view is that such a flood would produce too much water vapor for sunlight to reach the earth's surface. We would expect that a global flood would have left behind more geological and archaeological evidence. Then there is the logistical problem of the care and feeding of 42,000 animals for one year.

The language of Genesis 7:19-23 is open to other interpretations. Instead of covering the mountains, the Hebrew words used could refer to the mountains being drenched by the rain. Reference to all the earth could be understood as hyperbole or to all the earth in a particular area. In other words, we can't rule out the possibility that the flood was only regional in scope.

God has the ability to produce a flood of any magnitude. More important than the scope of the flood, however, is God's reason for sending it: He wanted to begin humanity again, this time starting with the most righteous man alive.

What actually happened is that instead of being drowned, sin got on the boat. This becomes clear when Noah and his family disembark. Noah became so drunk that he passed out, naked. While he was unconscious, one of his sons, Ham, came in and saw his father. Instead of preserving his father's dignity by quietly covering his body and keeping the matter to himself, Ham gossiped to his brothers.

This might not seem like much to us, but in the ancient Near East, seeing one's father's nakedness and joking about it would have been a serious offense to Noah's, and to the family's honor. The seriousness is clear from Noah's reaction when he learned what happened. He pronounced a curse on Ham's son, Canaan, a reference to the later Canaanites, those who would be living in the land Israel would inhabit. This whole scene may not sound as serious as one brother murdering another, but it reveals a painful reality: the sin problem hasn't been solved.

This news comes as no surprise to God. He already knew that the problem of sin was too serious to be solved by punishing the wicked. The spreading wickedness needed to be stopped in judgment. But God knew that sin was so pervasive it had tainted everyone, even a man as righteous as Noah (see Genesis 8:21). God already knew the flood would not solve the sin problem; now everyone else knew it.

Everyone hearing the story of the flood would realize that sin was serious. God was not just annoyed, like the gods in the Epic of Gilgamesh, He was pained at the effects of sin on His

masterpiece.   The sinful condition in every human heart—
original sin—as well as the sinful actions that flowed from those
sinful hearts, all of this grieved God's heart.

Something else is evident from hearing this story: God had
promised not to destroy the earth by flood. He even marked
that promise with a visible reminder, a rainbow. However God
chose to deal with the serious and pervasive problem of sin,
it would not be by destroying the earth. Apparently, He had
another way.

A noble, but failed attempt

We will learn about that other way in Genesis 12, but before
we get there, we must consider the Tower of Babel (Genesis
11). Some people in Mesopotamia had decided to establish
themselves as a city and build a tower to the heavens. God
interrupted their progress and scattered them across the earth.

Why did God stop them?   Was He threatened by human
accomplishment?   And how does this story fit into the larger
story of God's plan to repair the four broken relationships? Some
see the actions of these tower builders in a totally negative light,
one more example of human degradation. According to this
view, God stopped the builders to punish their pride.

I see it differently. I see the builders doing their best to heal the
four broken relationships. Notice that they try to build a tower
to the heavens. Many scholars consider this structure to be a
ziggurat, a sacred mountain. In the ancient world, mountain
tops were places of worship. Think Mount Olympus, home
of the gods according to the ancient Greeks. The higher the
elevation the closer one came to the gods. The tower builders
in Genesis 11 were trying to heal the breach they knew existed
between themselves and the gods.

Their tower-building efforts were also an attempt to "make a name" for themselves (Genesis 11:4). This suggests a desire for recognition, the need to leave one's mark on the world, a fear of being forgotten. While not sinful in themselves, these desires speak to a deeper need to find significance, to be at peace with who you are.

That the people in Babel come together in a city indicates their attempt to find reconciliation in the human-to-human realm. They knew they were made for community and didn't want to be "scattered over the face of the whole earth" (Genesis 11:4).

This desire to huddle together and avoid being scattered also suggests their alienation from the natural world. God had given humans the command to "fill the earth and subdue it" (Genesis 1:28). Yet here they were huddling together out of fear.

To their credit, they had developed some level of mastery over the earth as evidenced in their building techniques. They had learned to construct bricks and use tar to mortar the bricks together. Because they are made in God's image, they have the capacity to master their world; because they are fallen, they turn that mastery to their own ends, rather than to God's glory.

The builders of the Tower of Babel were attempting to restore these four broken relationships as best they knew how. They instinctively understood they were made to be at peace with God, with themselves, with each other, and with their world. The tower was their attempt to find that peace.

Every human being is still trying to do the same thing. Although we have been damaged by sin, the desire for these four relationships remains. Today we aren't joining together to build towers on the plains of Mesopotamia, but we are trying to find complete reconciliation.

We long for companionship, to be at peace with ourselves, to find purpose in our lives. Although we may not realize what we are longing for, we all want to be reconciled to God. "You have made us for yourself," prayed St. Augustine, "and our hearts are restless until they find their rest in you."

People have tried to calm this restlessness in many ways. Humans throughout history have tried to do so through religion. In our modern era, where many see religion as something to outgrow, the restlessness continues, as do the attempts to quiet it. Physical pleasures, material comforts, busyness, accomplishments, and acquisitions—we strive for rest.

What we find is just what the builders of the Tower of Babel would have found: it doesn't work. Even with our best efforts, humans cannot solve the sin problem on our own. This is why God stopped their project. He wasn't afraid they would succeed. He was concerned they would imagine they had succeeded when they had actually failed. The illusion of success, so evident in their mighty tower, would have been worse than failure.

The sin problem and resulting alienation needed to be solved. Sin was pervasive and universal, infecting even the most blameless man and his family. It was serious, creating violence and destruction wherever it went. Humans were incapable of solving the problem. If any solution was to be found, it would need to come from God. And so it did, but not in a way anyone could ever have expected. Prepare to be surprised on this next leg of our flight over the forest of Scripture.

Study Questions

1. We've described several ways we see broken relationships (human to God, human, self, nature) in these chapters. What other examples can you find?

2. Which of the three interpretations of Genesis 6:1-4 makes the most sense to you, and why? Can you think of another possible explanation?

3. Why might God have wanted His people to understand that the sin problem will require more than judgment?

4. Do you agree that every person is trying to restore the broken relationships in his or her life, whether they realize it or not? Why or why not?

Chapter Four

THE BEGINNING OF A NEW BEGINNING

Genesis 12-50

The hinge of the Bible

At first, God's plan to solve the sin problem seems absurd. If an entire community working together and utilizing the best of technology could not succeed, what chance has an elderly, childless couple? The difference is God. It is His plan, those involved are of His choosing, and His grace is in abundant supply.

God reveals His plan in the first three verses of Genesis 12:

> [1]The LORD had said to Abram, "Go from your country, your people and your father's household to the land I will show you. [2] I will make you into a great nation, and I will bless you; I will make your name great, and you will be a blessing. [3] I will bless those who bless you, and whoever curses you I will curse; and all peoples on earth will be blessed through you."

These verses are among the most important in all the Bible. You could even call them the "hinge" of the Bible. Up to this point we have learned how human sin spoiled God's creation. From this point forward, we will see God restore what sin destroyed. These verses mark the turning point.

This passage begins with a command: Abraham[1] is to leave behind his country, people and family and go to another land. God didn't tell him which land yet; that information would come later. This command is part of a covenant, a binding agreement between two parties. God initiated the agreement by issuing this command and making certain promises. Abraham must obey if he is to claim the promises.

There are several covenants in the Bible, such as the covenant God makes with Abraham in Genesis 15, with the Israelites on Mount Sinai (starting in Exodus 19), and with King David in 2 Samuel 7. The prophet, Jeremiah, predicted a "new covenant" (Jeremiah 31:31); at the Last Supper Jesus announced this new covenant had arrived (see Luke 22:20; Hebrews 8:8-12).

While one could see these as separate covenants, I think it's more accurate to see them as multiple expressions of a single covenant. All the covenants God makes from this time forward are a further unfolding of the one He makes with Abraham in Genesis 12. God's redemptive plan as contained in these three verses is at the heart of each new unfolding.

We can easily miss the magnitude of the sacrifice God commanded Abraham to make. His country, people, and family represented his world and everything in it. To leave one's country and live in another is no small thing, even today. Abraham had already begun this process, having moved at God's direction from Ur to Harran. As Abraham would discover, his journey had only begun.

To leave one's people group and family was an even bigger sacrifice. When we're with "our people" we know the language, values and other things so important they often go without saying. When we move to live among another people we must learn a whole new language, literally and figuratively.

---

[1] *The names of this important couple were originally Abram and Sarai until God renamed them Abraham and Sarah (see Genesis 17:1-8; 15-22). The meanings of the names don't change ("great father" and "princess" respectively). Most importantly, God changed them, indicating their special relationship with Him. We'll refer to them by their new names.*

Especially in Abraham's day, being with your people meant being with those you could depend on for protection and support. To live apart from your people left you vulnerable. This included physical vulnerability, but also economic. Engaging in everyday commerce comes with a risk if you are not among your own people. How can you be sure you're not getting ripped off? To whom do you turn if disaster strikes?

For Abraham to leave his people also meant changing his religious views. Abraham was raised to worship certain gods. These were identified with the territory and people group in which he lived. Both in Ur and Harran, the main god worshiped was Sîn, the moon god.

Now another god, Yahweh, had commanded Abraham to leave the land where Sîn was worshiped and go elsewhere. Changing one's gods was uncommon and risky. What if the former god was offended by this disloyalty? What if the new god proved unable to defend him?

God knew the tremendous step of faith He was calling Abraham to take. Perhaps this is why He committed Himself to Abraham in seven promises. The first was that Abraham would be the forefather of a "great nation." Ironically, Abraham and his wife, Sarah, had no children (see Genesis 11:30). Because they were old and childless, they weren't likely to have any. For this reason, Abraham had likely designated his nephew, Lot, as his heir. When he heard this first promise, Abraham probably assumed it would be fulfilled through Lot. He would eventually learn God had other plans.

The second promise was that God would bless Abraham. Such blessings would include many descendants and an enduring legacy, something highly desirable in those days. Other blessings would include prolific livestock, fertile fields, and profitable investments. Abraham would become a wealthy man, with "sheep and cattle, silver and gold, male and female servants, and camels and donkeys" (Genesis 24:35).

Third, God promised that He would make Abraham's name great. In other words, God would expand Abraham's reputation so that others would treat him with respect, as a man favored by God. This promise would have calmed at least some of Abraham's fears. People in those days would go out of their way to avoid offending someone who had been favored by the gods (see Genesis 21:22-23; 23:6).

God revealed something of His purpose in choosing Abraham in the next several promises. Fourth, Abraham would be blessed to be a blessing to others. We still talk about a person being a blessing to others, usually through some charitable action. In those days, to be a blessing included that and more.

Fifth, Abraham's name would be used to bless others. "May you be as blessed as Abraham" was more than wishful thinking, but was believed to make a positive difference for the one to whom it was spoken. It would be as if Abraham's life was so filled with blessing that when you invoked his name, some of his blessings spilled out to benefit others.

Still more wonderful, in His sixth promise God said He would bless those who blessed Abraham and curse those who cursed him. These words demonstrate God's special care for Abraham since He took it on Himself to personally bless and curse. Those who blessed Abraham by befriending him, doing business with him, favoring him in decisions, becoming his allies, and in any other way would find they'd made a very good investment. He was someone you wanted to get to know because he had a Friend in very high places.

To curse Abraham, that is to ridicule, mock, or dismiss him, was definitely not a good idea. God promised to make life miserable for that person, dishing out punishment much worse than anything Abraham had to endure. To be a source of blessing and someone you don't want to curse provided Abraham with divine protection.

The seventh promise is the best of all. God promised that through Abraham all nations (or more literally, "all families of the ground") will be blessed (see Genesis 12:3). God may have chosen to speak of the "ground" as a way to echo the curse made against the ground in Genesis 3. We'll come back to this in a moment.

In this final promise we have the gospel in a nutshell. If that sounds like an overstatement, listen to what Peter says as he preaches in Jerusalem (see Acts 3:25). After proclaiming Jesus as the Messiah, he reminds his audience of Jews that they are "heirs of the prophets and of the covenant God made with your fathers." They are the descendants of Abraham; this is the great nation God had promised him. Peter continues by quoting from Genesis 12:3: "Through your offspring all peoples on earth will be blessed." What God promised Abraham was fulfilled through Jesus.

If Peter's words aren't clear enough, we have those of the Apostle Paul in his letter to the Galatians. This church was made up primarily of Gentiles, that is, non-Jews, those described in the phrase, "all peoples on earth." Paul asserts that the Gentiles who come to God by faith in Christ will be made right with God. To prove his point, Paul quotes from Genesis 12:3: "Scripture foresaw that God would justify the Gentiles by faith, and announced the gospel in advance to Abraham: 'All nations will be blessed through you'" (Galatians 3:8). There it is: this seventh promise is "the gospel in advance"!

Earlier we suggested God's reference to "all families of the ground" may have been alluding to Genesis 3 where God cursed the ground because of the sin of Adam and Eve. That possibility grows stronger as we compare these two passages.

In Genesis 3, Adam and Eve grasped at what was not theirs only to lose what they had. Abraham, by contrast, released what he possessed—nation, people, family—only to gain much more. Adam and Eve sought to become "like God, knowing good and evil" (Genesis 3:5). By contrast, Abraham voluntarily surrendered to God's will. Instead of knowledge, Abraham received promises. He was not even told where he was going, only that God would show him (see Genesis 12:1).

At the same time, through his obedience, Abraham did gain a knowledge of good and evil. He came to know God in a way no one had known Him before. And he entered on a path that allowed him to discover good and avoid evil, so long as he obeyed.

By their choices, Adam and Eve ruptured the four key relationships: with God, with each other, with self, and with creation. Abraham, by contrast voluntarily surrendered his relationship with those closest to him, except for Sarah and Lot. He also put himself in a situation where intra-personal alienation would be likely, forfeiting his identity and security.

Abraham had made himself at home in his world with a nice livelihood in the cities of Ur and Harran. Now he surrendered this settled existence for a new life as a nomad. He voluntarily ruptured his relationship with the world, making it necessary to learn a new way of living.

Why did he make these drastic choices, disrupting three of the four key relationships? For the sake of the primary relationship: human to God. Abraham invested in this relationship, even if it meant sacrificing the other three.

While Adam and Eve's decision cost them full-fledged harmony, Abraham's sacrifice strengthened his relationship with God. It also strengthened all of the other relationships as well. He became wealthy in his new life as a nomad, his immediate family miraculously expanded, and he gained a new identity as God's covenant partner; he and Sarah were renamed by God.

The actions of Adam and Eve represented a terrible example of disobedience, one that brought disaster on themselves and every other human. Abraham's actions, though purchased at the price of sacrificial obedience, brought blessing not only to himself but to "all peoples on earth" (Genesis 12:3).

Even though they had only known God's faithfulness, Adam and Eve refused to believe God's word and character, allowing themselves to be confused by the Deceiver. Abraham heard God's voice as something strange, having been raised to follow a different god. Yet when he heard what God said to him, he believed it and acted on his faith. No wonder the Apostle Paul referred to Abraham as the father of all believers (see Romans 4:16).

To say he was the father of all believers means that Abraham is our example for how to live by faith. It also means that Abraham is the pioneer of this life of faith. He didn't just model great faith, he made it possible for the rest of us to live by faith, carving out the path we follow.

We can also say that Abraham is the archetype of our faith. Engineers build an archetype or prototype to understand how best to make all future models. In literature and psychology, archetype is used to describe a recurrent pattern followed by others. Abraham is our archetype; the life of every believer follows his pattern. We don't just choose to follow his example; his example is the paradigm for the life of faith.

God is like a kindergarten teacher

The rest of Genesis describes the initial outworking of God's plan in the life of Abraham. There we learn about his children, grandchildren, and great-grandchildren. To be more precise, the rest of Genesis focuses our attention on one of his sons, Isaac, one of his grandsons, Jacob, and twelve of his great-grandsons, the sons of Jacob.

Since the first of God's promises to Abraham is to make him into a great nation, we might have thought that the next several chapters would describe the rapid growth of offspring who would number in the tens of thousands by the end of Genesis. Instead, the growth of Abraham's family was very slow; by the end of the book he only had about 70 descendants through Isaac and Jacob.

This is one of many clues that God is up to something more than multiplication. More than producing lots of descendants, God was interested in ensuring that Abraham's descendants understood Him: who He is, how He works, and what He values.

God behaved here like a kindergarten teacher. He recognized that Abraham and his descendants were new to all this but He has a lot to teach them about Himself. He began with basic lessons, repeated those lessons as needed, and advanced to more difficult assignments when His students were ready.

What are some of the lessons He wanted them to learn? For one, they must learn that He is in charge. He chooses which of Abraham's offspring will carry on the covenant plan. Ishmael was as much Abraham's son as Isaac, but God chose Isaac as next in line. Esau was Isaac's first son, but God decided to use Jacob instead. It wasn't that God didn't love Ishmael or Esau, but He wanted His people to understand that He has the right to choose.

Through the centuries, people have tried to say there was something wrong with Ishmael or that Abraham failed to trust God, and that was why God chose Isaac instead. Some even blame Abraham for the conflict between Jews (descended from Isaac) and Muslims (descended from Ishmael).

This reads way too much into the story and actually overlooks all the positive things the Bible says about Ishmael. People tend to do the same with Esau, making him to be worse than he is.

Criticizing those not chosen and celebrating those who are not only misreads the Bible, but runs the risk of missing the lesson God wanted to teach His people. He wanted them to understand that He has the right to do things His way. This is one way He shows His mercy and power.

In Abraham's culture, the firstborn son was thought to have inherited the majority of the father's strength. This was why most of the father's inheritance went to the firstborn son, the remainder being distributed among the other sons. God chose not to follow this practice, known as primogeniture. He gets to choose whom to include.

Primogeniture was just one of the cultural values God chose to set aside; polytheism, child sacrifice, excessive violence are others. God moved His people beyond these values in their understanding and practices. Like a good teacher, God began where His students were to bring them to where He wanted them to be.

God chose ordinary people, not perfect ones. These chapters describe God's people doing things they shouldn't have done. Out of fear, Abraham lied to the Egyptians about his wife being his sister; he did the same thing later when among the Canaanites. Sarah actually laughed in disbelief when she learned she would become pregnant. Isaac and Rebekah both played favorites, each preferring one of their twin sons over the other. One of those twins, Jacob, was deceitful, tricking his own brother out of his rights. Joseph had an arrogant streak that grated on his brothers' nerves. God did not ignore these faults but worked to remove them over time.

Part of the reason God chose ordinary people was to demonstrate His extraordinary power. Had God chosen to work only with superheroes, His own power might be missed and later generations of ordinary followers would think themselves off the hook. Instead, God chose very ordinary people like Abraham, Sarah, Jacob, and Joseph and helped them do amazing things.

Part of why God chose to use these particular people is known only to God. It's not that Ishmael, Esau, or Joseph's brothers were unsuitable, either too much like superheroes, or too flawed to flourish. They might have done just as well as those who were chosen.

God was demonstrating His right to choose. There is plenty of mystery here, but there is also a lesson in plain sight. This is God's classroom and He gets to decide which students to work with, when, and how. While never unfair in His choices—that would be very ungodlike—God remains free to do things His way.

The faith it took Abraham and Sarah to leave Harran is amazing; so too is their perseverance to wait decades for God to fulfill His promise of a son (see Genesis 21). Then we watch in amazement as Abraham finds the courage to offer this son as a sacrifice at God's request (see Genesis 22). Thankfully, God's request was only a test, but Abraham didn't know this as he raised his knife. When we see what ordinary people can accomplish with God's help, we realize how God's power shows up best in ordinary people.

That God didn't tell Abraham this was a test is only one example—albeit a dramatic one—of how God often reserved important information until just the right time. At first, He didn't even tell Abraham and Sarah that the nation they would create would come from a child to be borne by Sarah.

God allowed them to believe that Lot would be their heir, but then Lot moved away (see Genesis 13). After Lot left, God told Abraham he would father the heir (see Genesis 15). Since Sarah could not conceive, Abraham reasoned he should take another wife, Hagar, and through her produce a son, Ishmael (see Genesis 16). Finally, after another decade or so, God told Abraham that Ishmael wouldn't be the heir; the heir would be Sarah's child (see Genesis 17). He could have told them this way back in Genesis 12, but waited more than two decades to do so.

Sounds like a teacher, doesn't it? Rather than blurting out on the first day all that needs to be learned through the year, the teacher waits, prepares the pupils, strengthens their capacity, and when they're ready, presents what they need to know.

The most important subject in God's classroom is faith. He wants His people to obey; obedience is essential but must arise from faith. God didn't tell them everything, just what they needed to know. Then He gave them the opportunity to put what they know into action. When they did, they usually found themselves up against an obstacle. By persevering in their faith, they saw God work in spite of the obstacle, which further strengthened their faith.

A great illustration of this teaching technique can be seen in how God provided children for His people. After all, one of God's first promises to this childless couple was that they would have a nation of offspring. Right away, however, we discover an obstacle: Sarah can't have children. If God intended to produce a nation, a childless couple is a curious way to begin. But more than offspring, God wants offspring who know how to trust, so He chose a couple for whom even having one son was going to take a miracle.

God will teach this same lesson several more times using barren women: Abraham's daughter-in-law, Rebekah, and Rebekah's two daughters-in-law, Leah and Rachel. Building a nation through barren women seems a ridiculous plan, until you realize God's purpose is primarily to build a faith-filled nation.

The next several books of the Old Testament reveal God continuing this work as teacher. As we fly over this next section of the Bible, we will see how He increasingly unfolds the plans He began with Abraham, transforming a family into a nation and then leading that nation to its homeland.

Study Questions

1. In your own words, explain why Genesis 12:1-3 is considered the "hinge" of the Bible.

2. What would it be like for God to call you to take a step of faith similar to the one He required of Abraham?

3. Do you agree that Ishmael and Esau might have been just as useful to God, had He chosen them? Why or why not?

4. What other lessons might God have been trying to teach His "class" of new students?

Chapter Five

THE BEGINNING OF A NEW NATION

Exodus - Deuteronomy

An unlikely plan

God's plan to solve the problem of sin seems to have hit a snag. The plan began when God promised to bless Abraham and Sarah with descendants and much more. This couple did become wealthy and influential and, by a miracle, had been able to have a son. After a century or two, their descendants through Isaac and Jacob numbered almost six dozen, not quite the nation God had promised.

Even worse, their brief sojourn in the land of Canaan, the land God had promised to Abraham, was now over. Because of a serious famine in Canaan they had moved to Egypt.

While it looks like God's plan has hit a snag, it hasn't. All this is part of His plan; God had even predicted to Abraham, "for four hundred years your descendants will be strangers in a country not their own and . . . will be enslaved and mistreated there. But I will punish the nation they serve as slaves, and afterward they will come out with great possessions" (Genesis 15:13-14).

The book of Exodus describes how God fulfilled this promise. Not only did He deliver the Israelites from Egyptian slavery, God used this experience to shape them into the promised nation. The first half of Exodus describes the exciting events that led to their freedom. The last half of the book contains the essence of the law He gave them, less exciting in some ways, but just as important.

When the book of Exodus opens, God's people are right where He predicted they would be, "strangers in a country not their own" (Genesis 15:13). They were not yet slaves, but they were becoming increasingly unwelcome in Egypt.

It isn't likely the Israelites had ever been wholly embraced by the Egyptians, even though the Egyptians owed a great deal to these immigrants. Many Egyptian lives had been preserved through the great famine referenced earlier because of an Israelite, Joseph, whom God had elevated from prisoner to prime minister (see Genesis 37-50).

Even in Joseph's day, the Egyptians preferred to keep their distance from the Israelites, partly because of cultural differences (see Genesis 43:32; 46:34). There were also differences in religion. Egyptians worshiped a vast number of gods while the Israelites worshiped only one. Egyptian worship was focused on the afterlife, an aspect of religion to which the Israelites paid scant attention.

What brought the Israelites to the Egyptians' attention and fearfully so, was their growth in numbers. For some reason, the Israelites had begun to multiply like rabbits. The growth rate was so remarkable the Egyptians attributed it to something supernatural. They were right.

God had chosen this moment to grow the Israelites into a nation-sized group of people. This population explosion also served a second divine purpose, prompting the Egyptians to respond in fear.

Ancient Egyptians were very religious, so when they saw something happening that was humanly impossible, like this dramatic growth in population, they assumed it was the work of the gods. Furthermore, if this burgeoning Israelite population chose to ally themselves with one of Egypt's enemies, Egypt would be in trouble (see Exodus 1:10).

We see Egypt's growing sense of fear in their response to Israelite growth. First, they forced the Israelites to work on Pharaoh's construction projects (see Exodus 1:11). When this didn't slow the growth rate but actually increased it, they worked them harder (see Exodus 1:12-14).

Then the Egyptians turned to infanticide. They commanded the Israelite midwives to kill every Israelite baby boy at birth (see Exodus 1:15-21). Thanks to the courage of these midwives, this strategy failed, prompting the Egyptians to became even more desperate. They authorized *any* Egyptian to kill *any* Israelite infant boy (see Exodus 1:22).

Israel's supernatural growth and Egypt's increasingly desperate fear set the scene for the deliverance to come. The Egyptian response made it impossible for the Israelites to safely remain, but how could the Israelites escape except through a miracle?

No surprise, God's miracle started small with an Israelite infant boy named Moses. Hidden in the Nile by his mother, Moses was found by an Egyptian princess who adopted him and raised him in the palace. Aware of his true lineage, Moses sought to help the Israelites but made such a mess of things, including committing murder, he had to flee for his life. He finally landed in the country of Midian where he got a job as a shepherd (and married the boss' daughter) (see Exodus 2:1-15).

A baby boy adopted by Egyptians, a would-be savior who committed murder, a fugitive middle-aged shepherd living many miles from Egypt . . . this hardly sounds like someone who would become an instrument of God's miraculous deliverance. But remember, God likes to work with ordinary people to do extraordinary things.

When He assigned Moses the task of leading the Israelites out of Egypt, God made clear that the Israelites are His people. Yahweh knows they are suffering. He has "seen" their misery and "heard" their cries. Filled with concern, God has come down to rescue His people and take them to the land He had promised them. And Moses would be the one to lead them (see Exodus 3:7-10).

When Moses resisted this assignment, citing his (very real) inadequacies, God assured him it would turn out all right, because He would be with him. God's presence would make all the difference (see Exodus 3:12). Once again, we see the significance of the human to God relationship. Because God was with Moses and the Israelites, He would transform them from a bunch of discouraged slaves into a nation on the move. They would find the courage to face down Egyptian might, both human and supernatural, and they would carry out the mission God had assigned them.

The Israelites would need God's presence because, as He made clear to Moses at the burning bush, Pharaoh would not let them go without a fight. And what a fight it was! It started small but ended up deadly and catastrophic. It brought about Israel's release, but accomplished more beside.

Celestial smack-down

We refer to this fight as the "ten plagues," because God supernaturally afflicted the Egyptians over a series of months with ten natural/supernatural disasters. These disasters were sent to persuade Pharaoh to let the Israelites leave Egypt. The king continued to resist Moses' demand until he and his country were brought to their knees.

Liberating the Israelites was one purpose for the plagues, but they accomplished more. Had God only wanted to deliver the Israelites, one plague would have been sufficient, one devastating blow that rendered Egypt powerless to respond.

Why did God choose to bring about this deliverance using ten plagues, each growing progressively more severe and each targeting a different aspect of Egyptian culture? For one thing, God wanted to demonstrate that His power was greater than that of the Egyptian gods, a kind of "celestial smack-down."

Most of the plagues connect with particular Egyptian deities. When God turned the waters of the Nile to blood (see Exodus 7:14-25), He demonstrated His power over Anuket and Hapi, deities associated with the Nile River. The plague of frogs (see Exodus 8:1-15) did the same with the frog-headed goddess, Heqet, responsible for fertility and childbirth.

Plagues that involved something rising from the ground, like the plague of gnats (see Exodus 8:16-19), challenged the Egyptian earth god, Geb. Plagues that descended from the sky, like the plague of hail (see Exodus 9:13-35), challenged the sky goddess, Nut. The plague afflicting livestock (see Exodus 9:1-12) challenged the many Egyptian gods and goddess associated with domestic animals, like the bull and ram.

In the two final plagues we see most clearly how they targeted Egyptian deities. The three-day blackening of the sun (see Exodus 10:21-29) was aimed at discrediting the sun god, Re (or Ra), king of the Egyptian gods, source of life, and closely associated with Pharaoh. That the eclipse didn't affect the territory of the Israelites only strengthened God's point.

The final plague was the final straw (see Exodus 11; 12:29-30). The death of the first-born son in every Egyptian household crippled Egyptian culture. Remember, first-born sons were thought to possess the lion's share of their father's strength. Overnight, Egypt's future was decimated.

Even more significant, the Egyptians considered Pharaoh to be a god. The death of his eldest son (see Exodus 12:29) not only showed Yahweh's power over the king but broke the line of succession. Israel's God had decimated Egypt's gods.

Whether or not each disaster was aimed at a particular deity, the plagues demonstrated Yahweh's power over Egyptians society, the well-being of which was the responsibility of Egypt's gods. Egyptians were very proud of their society and very concerned that it functioned like a healthy body. Because of Israel's God, that body was on the ropes.

God didn't hate the Egyptians. They were guilty of oppressing and enslaving His people and needed to be punished, but God loved Israel's enemies. He wanted them to understand the truth. He even welcomed those Egyptians who chose to leave their land and way of life and become part of Israel (see Exodus 12:38).

Those Egyptians who didn't leave were happy to see the Israelites go. They had become terrified of these immigrants, a terror produced as they witnessed how much greater Israel's God was than all the gods of Egypt. They even provided Israel with parting gifts like silver, gold, and clothing (see Exodus 12:35-36). This wealth would be used to provide for the coming journey and later, in the construction of Israel's tabernacle. You might even say this was back pay for all those years of servitude and slavery.

It was important that the Israelites be eyewitnesses of Egypt's humiliation. They had spent all their lives as immigrants in Egypt, so had their parents, and their parents' parents, and their parents' parents' parents, and beyond. The image of Egypt as great and themselves as weak outsiders was indelibly stamped on their psyches. To remove that impression would take a miracle, actually ten of them.

They needed to see Egypt humiliated in order to understand God and their relationship with Him. He had said the Israelites were His chosen people whom He loved. He had promised He would curse those who curse them (see Genesis 12:3) and punish the nation that oppressed them (see Genesis 15:14). They had heard He was "the Judge of all the earth" who could be counted on to do the right thing (see Genesis 18:25). By punishing the Egyptians, God reinforced Israel's identity as His people and His own character as a just God who keeps His promises.

There is another reason why the Israelites needed to witness Egypt's humiliation. Egyptian culture was hyper-religious, with grand temples and elaborate rituals, myriad gods and goddesses, powerful priests, a divine king, every aspect of life connected with religion, and life itself considered preparation for the afterlife.

Imagine being an Israelite growing up in this kind of environment. You only have a single god, no temple, few rituals, the bare outlines of theology, no concept of the afterlife, and not even a physical image of your god. The temptation to admire, envy, even adopt Egyptian religion must have been powerful. The plagues were God's way of making clear which religion was right.

But why did the plagues start small and grow increasingly severe? The answer to this question takes us closer to one of God's less obvious purposes for the plagues. These plagues didn't just humble Pharaoh's heart, they hardened it. With each plague, God offered Pharaoh a choice. Every time the king chose to resist, he hardened his heart, making it easier to resist and harder to obey the next time.

In certain passages, we are told that Pharaoh hardened his own heart. In others, we are told that God hardened Pharaoh's heart.

Both are true. God presented the king with a choice; built into that choice, as into every choice, is the solidifying of resolve. The right choice makes the next good choice easier and the next wrong choice harder. The wrong choice makes the next wrong choice easier and the next right choice harder. Over and over, Pharaoh made the wrong choice, which hardened his heart.

Why would God want Pharaoh's heart to harden? Doesn't He want everyone to repent? Yes, He does, and would have preferred to see Pharaoh willingly release the Israelites. Given the mindset of the Egyptians, particularly Pharaoh, this was unlikely. Even so, God gave Pharaoh choices, starting with less serious plagues. Pharaoh, being Pharaoh, did the rest.

A hard-hearted Pharaoh served God's purposes well. It was Pharaoh's hard heart that allowed the situation to get so bad it clearly demonstrated Yahweh's superiority. Pharaoh's hard heart allowed the situation to deteriorate to the point that Pharaoh had no choice but to release the Israelites.

It was Pharaoh's hard heart that made him quickly regret his decision and send his army after the Israelites to destroy them. It was Pharaoh's hard heart that chose unwisely to pursue the Israelites into the midst of a temporarily parted sea. It was Pharaoh's hard heart that drowned the Egyptian army. And only if the Egyptian army was destroyed could Israel travel through the wilderness and spend a necessary season unmolested at Mount Sinai.

God's gift of the law

If the first half of the book of Exodus describes how God took Israel out of Egypt, the second half concerns how God took Egypt out of Israel. He began this process earlier by revealing His greatness; it would continue at Sinai by showing Israel theirs. In order to see themselves as God's chosen nation, they must now understand themselves as something more than slaves.

How God chose to accomplish this make-over may surprise you: He gave them a law. That seems counterintuitive; how can a law liberate? Slaves need rules, not laws. They don't deserve laws (in the mind of their owners, that is), because they're only slaves. But a law is essential for a nation chosen by God, a nation given a great mission. A law would protect this important nation and keep it pointed toward its God-ordained goal. To have a law is to be made noble.

To have this particular law, the law revealed by God to Moses at Sinai and unfolded in Exodus, Leviticus, Numbers, and Deuteronomy, would be a tremendously ennobling gift. Contrary to popular belief, God did not give the Israelites the law of Moses to discourage them by showing them they couldn't keep it. They knew that what He had commanded them was "not too difficult" or beyond their reach (Deuteronomy 30:11-14).

This explains why the Israelites loved the law. The longest chapter in the whole Bible, Psalm 119, is all about the greatness of the law. Every reference to the law in the Old Testament is positive. The Israelites knew they were tremendously privileged to have been given the law and thanked God for it.

There are passages in the New Testament that appear to contrast the law with grace, as if the two are mutually exclusive. As we will see when we look at God's plan in the epistles, such a view is a serious misreading.

Another popular misconception is that God gave the law so that by keeping it the Israelites would become His people. In other words, they would be "saved" by their works. But they already were God's people *before* they received the law. God rescued them from Egypt and brought them to Sinai *because* they were His people.

They became God's people, as Christians become God's people, by grace through faith, not by works. Abraham was chosen by grace and followed by faith. God didn't wait until the New Testament to relate to people by grace through faith. He has always worked this way.

This law was given, not to make them God's people, but to teach them how God's people should live. Set free from their mindset of slavery, they could now discover the freedom that comes from living in the image of God, in harmony with God, with each other, with self, and with creation.

The law was part of the curriculum employed by God the teacher. Through the law they learned they were in covenant with God; He was their King and they were His people (see Leviticus 26:12). As their King, He deserved their sacrifices and especially, their obedience.

They continued to learn the importance of living by faith. Prohibited from representing Him in a physical way, they followed an invisible God. God Himself provided a pillar of cloud by day and a pillar of fire by night to guide them on the path from Egypt to the promised land of Canaan. They even had to rely on Him for their water and their food.

God taught them about His holiness. He could only be approached in the prescribed way: through those appointed to represent Him, the priests, at the appointed place, the tabernacle, and in the appointed ways, through the rituals. Trespassing on God's holiness could be very dangerous (see Exodus 19:12-13).

God as a bicyclist in Mozambique

God not only revealed Himself as a teacher, He also made Himself known in another way. This way reminds me of a bicyclist in Mozambique. A missionary had driven to the remote northern part of that African country. His car's fan belt broke, leaving him stranded hundreds of miles from the nearest auto parts store. Along came a Mozambican man on a bicycle. The bicyclist stopped at the stranded vehicle, learned of the problem, and quickly fashioned a fan belt from one of the inner tubes on his own bike. This work-around was good enough to get the missionary back to a place where he could purchase a fan belt.

God is like that bicyclist in Mozambique. He knows we're living in a fallen world and for that reason will be unable to experience ultimate wholeness. Because He cares about us, He provides us with "work-arounds," solutions that temporarily fix the problem until He brings the ultimate solution to pass.

The law contains lots of these "work-arounds" which allow God's people to find some measure of reconciliation in the four broken relationships. We can see this most clearly in the core section of the law, what we know as the Ten Commandments (see Exodus 20 and Deuteronomy 5). These can be divided into two parts, the first describing how to love God, the last how to love each other.

Humans were made for fellowship with God, so He explained in His law how they could most fully experience His presence in this fallen world. They were to build Him a palace right in the middle of their camp. This palace would be portable so they could carry it with them and set it up wherever they camped. Much of the law concerns how to experience the blessings of God's presence in His palace, what we know as the tabernacle.

The law explained how people could live together in peace, navigating the inevitable tensions that arise. It told them how to love their neighbors and even their enemies. It described how someone alienated from the community, whether through disobedience or disease, could be restored to fellowship.

Through the law they could experience a measure of intrapersonal reconciliation. Israel's neighbors experienced chronic insecurity in their relationship with their gods who were notorious for not clearly revealing their expectations. As a result, their worshipers couldn't be sure they had done enough. Even worse, these other religions involved multiple gods and spiritual beings; humans might be the target of a curse or some divine displeasure, you just didn't know.

By contrast, obedience to the law allowed God's people to live in *shalom* (peace, wholeness), confident they had done what they could to please Him. God had, so to speak, laid His cards on the table. He made clear what was required and how He would treat obedience and disobedience.

To live by God's law allowed them to become more reconciled to a fallen creation. For example, the laws regarding Sabbath— resting every seventh day—demonstrate how to make the most of one's work in this world. Through the law the Israelites learned how they could maintain the productivity of their land by letting their fields lie fallow once every seven years. The law showed how to provide a measure of economic fairness by forgiving debts every fifty years.

Through all these laws God sought to change how the Israelites thought about themselves. He helped them, like a good teacher, to understand more clearly about Himself and their role. He also provided work-arounds so they could experience the fullest possible measure of reconciliation in the four broken relationships.

God had promised Abraham that his descendants would form a nation and take possession of a land of their own. Through Moses, God had liberated this nation from captivity and provided them with a law. But this nation still needed a land in which to live. How will these former slaves ever be able to conquer another nation and take possession of their land? The next leg of our flight over the forest of Scripture will reveal the answer.

Study Questions

1. This chapter mentions several purposes for the 10 plagues. Which purpose stands out most in your mind and why? Can you think of other purposes for the plagues?

2. Do you agree with my explanation of the hardening of Pharaoh's heart? Why or why not?

3. What do you think of my explanation of the law being a source of Israel's liberation?

4. What other work-arounds can you see in the material we've covered thus far?

Chapter Six

THE PROMISED LAND
Joshua - Ruth

Into the Promised Land

Just over there, across the Jordan River, lay Israel's land. God had promised this territory to Abraham years before and repeated that promise many times since. Through Moses, God had led the Israelites to the doorstep of the promised land. Their destiny as a nation that would bless all other nations lay just across the Jordan River. All they needed to do was move in and settle down.

Unfortunately, God had brought them to this point during the season when the Jordan overflowed its banks. This river, easily forded most of the year, now flowed as a mile-wide torrent.

To make matters worse, awaiting them on the other side were people who considered this land their own and who were unwilling to give it up without a fight. Nor was Moses leading the Israelites. Joshua, their new commander, had great potential but had never faced a challenge like this. Either this was a huge disaster in the making, or God's school of faith was still in session.

The Book of Joshua opens with God's reassuring words to Joshua: I will be with you and keep My promises to My people, but you must obey Me (see Joshua 1:2-6, 9). In one way, these words echo God's reassurance to Moses at the burning bush (see Exodus 3:12; 4:12).

In another way, God's message to Joshua was quite different. Yes, Joshua was to obey God, but specifically, he was to obey the law God had spoken through Moses (see Joshua 1:7-8). You could say a page had been turned in Israel's education.

Prior to Moses, God had spoken to His people directly, but periodically. He appeared to Abraham and one of his descendants with a particular message. With Moses, those conversations occurred more frequently and even more directly; the Bible describes God speaking to Moses "face to face" (Exodus 33:11).

On Mount Sinai, God gave to Moses the law that established how the Israelites were to live as God's people. After this, Moses clarified, taught, supplemented, and reinforced the law, helping the Israelites understand and adjust themselves to God's requirements.

With Moses, the lawgiver, dead, the law became the embodiment of God's teaching among the Israelites. Those who would lead God's people, beginning with Joshua, would be measured by how well they obeyed this law and helped Israel do the same.

This feels like God was moving further from His people. Before He had spoken directly, but now has recorded His words for future generations. How was this helping heal the broken relationship between humans and God?

Actually, the giving of the law was one of God's greatest work-arounds. By making known His will once and for all, anyone could understand what God wanted, what happens when one obeyed and when one disobeyed. They still had a leader, Joshua, and those tasked with teaching and interpreting the law, the priests and Levites. Like a good teacher, God was now putting more responsibility into the hands of the pupils to teach themselves.

Learning to live by faith

One thing hadn't changed, God's emphasis on the importance

of living by faith. He even employed a guest instructor: Rahab. This prostitute from Jericho is one of the greatest examples of faith, not only in the Book of Joshua but in the whole Bible. She confessed her belief that God is sovereign over nature, over powerful people, over other nations, and over every other god. She also affirmed that God is gracious, willing to be merciful to Israel and even to her (see Joshua 2:9-13).

Even more than confessing her faith, she acted on it, shifting her loyalty to Yahweh from the gods she had been raised to worship. And she did this under threat of death at the hands of the king of Jericho and before she received any assurance of safety from the spies taking refuge in her home. Her remarkable faith made a huge difference. It strengthened the faith of the spies, Joshua, and all Israel. Her faith also saved her life, the lives of her family, and the lives of many Israelites.

No wonder Rahab's faith has been celebrated by so many for so long. Joshua allowed her a place among the Israelites. Later, Jewish teachers called her an ideal proselyte whose profession of faith resembled that of Moses. Several New Testament authors used her as an example of faith to be emulated (see James 2:25 and Hebrews 11:31). God admired her so much He allowed her to become an ancestress of King David and Jesus Himself (see Matthew 1:1-5).

God gave the Israelites a chance to learn about faith at the banks of the flooded Jordan River. Any other time of the year, the Jordan would be a minor obstacle, easily forded. But now, at the worst possible time, God told them to cross. The priests were instructed to lift the Ark of the Covenant, an important piece of tabernacle furniture meant to represent God's throne, and step into the flooded river.

To their credit, they obeyed. When they did, "the waters from upstream stopped flowing" (Joshua 3:16). What they didn't know when they obeyed was that God had already blocked the waters upstream. The moment the priests stepped into the river, the flow ceased. You might call it a miracle of timing. Just when they needed it, the river bed became a dry road across which the Israelites could pass into their new homeland.

Sound familiar? God produced at the Jordan River a variation on the crossing of the Red Sea. Apparently, He wanted miracles to mark both Israel's departure from slavery and entry into freedom. In both cases, God's people had to act: Moses had to hold out his hand over the water (see Exodus 14:21) and the priests had to step into the water (see Joshua 3:15).

Neither miracle was instantaneous; in both, the waters receded gradually. Both took place by natural means at a divine command: God sent a strong east wind to blow on the Red Sea all night (see Exodus 14:21); God likely blocked the Jordan with a mudslide, known to occur in that area (see Joshua 3:16). Both required the Israelites to step into what had been a dangerous place just a short while earlier, demonstrating their belief in God's power and goodness on their behalf.

Another lesson on faith awaited the Israelites once they crossed the Jordan River. They would need to be circumcised. Circumcision, the removal of the foreskin from the male penis, was the distinguishing mark for all Israelite men dating back to Abraham's day. But this ritual act had been neglected by the Israelites; the men who entered Canaan were not properly circumcised.

God had not confronted them about this before, but He could hardly allow them to begin their conquest of the promised land as His people unless they were His fully devoted followers. All the men would need to be circumcised.

As you can imagine, this is a painful and debilitating operation. You would only voluntarily immobilize your army someplace safe, far from the enemy, right? Wrong! God waited until they had arrived in enemy territory to command circumcision. What better way to teach the Israelites to trust in God's protection.

One of God's most powerful lessons on faith came from the land itself. God had brought them to a particular place on the map. Think of it, God owns all lands and could have given His people any land He chose. Why Canaan?

Take it from me, this is a beautiful land. But it has its drawbacks, one of them being a limited water supply. Large quantities of fresh water can be found in the Sea of Galilee and the Jordan River, but both of these are located deep in the Rift Valley. Diverting water from either source up to tillable soil would have been impossible for ancient Israel.

Water isn't a problem in Mesopotamia where Abraham came from. This land, named "between the rivers," is also known as the Fertile Crescent. Water is also plentiful in Egypt, the land of the Nile, from which they had recently escaped. There was so much water there and the ground so easily worked it was said you could dig a canal with your big toe (see Deuteronomy 11:10).

Instead, God took Israel to Canaan, "a land of mountains and valleys that drinks rain from heaven" (Deuteronomy 11:11). He did this so they would learn to trust Him for rain and everything else they needed.

God chose this land for another reason. It formed a land bridge that joined three continents. All land travel between Africa, Europe, and Asia would have to cross this narrow bridge. Imagine the potential influence of the nation that possessed this land. Think of the blessings they could bring to all other nations.

The principle of retribution

Faith was an important lesson in God's curriculum. Another was the principle of retribution. The principle can be expressed this way:

Obedience brings blessing;
Disobedience brings disaster.

We see the positive side, obedience brings blessing, demonstrated in Israel's defeat of Jericho as they obeyed God's unorthodox battle plan (see Joshua 6). The negative side is well illustrated by what happened to Achan and his family as a result of stealing some of the goods set apart for destruction (see Joshua 7). Most of the Book of Judges illustrates the results of disobedience.

Violence in the Book of Joshua

In the Book of Joshua, the promised blessings include victory in battle leading to possession of the land. While this certainly advances God's plan to establish the nation of Israel, it seems to contradict God's promise to use Israel to bless all nations. It's hard to bless others with a raised sword in your hand. It's hard to reconcile the violence in the Old Testament, particularly in the Book of Joshua, with a God of love.

It helps if we read the conquest accounts first, in their historical context and, second, in light of what we know to be true of God's character and plan. When we read these accounts in their historical context, we realize that the ancient world was a violent place. God stepped into this culture to develop His plan, adapting His approach to what He found there.

God didn't step into a violent culture because He prefers violence. In fact, He did so to reduce the violence. Israel's law called for less violence and greater justice than the laws of its neighbors.

Thanks in part to God's work through His people, our world has become increasingly less violent. Ironically, contemporary indignation at God's violence results largely from God Himself, who has used the Judeo-Christian tradition to steer humanity away from violence toward peace.

The ancient world was not only violent, but also commonly employed exaggeration when describing battles. Ancient kings commonly used hyperbole to tell of their victories, which means that anyone hearing a battle account in those days would expect exaggeration. So, when the Bible describes God commanding the annihilation of entire people groups (see Deuteronomy 7:1-2) and Israel obeying that command (see Joshua 10:40-42; 11:12), reading in historical context means assuming these accounts employ hyperbole.

Actually, finding passages in the Bible that describe the annihilation of Israel's enemies is not easy. A close reading reveals that Israel's primary weapon was not its sword, but fear of its sword. The prevailing verb used to describe the conquest is not killed, but "drove out." Even the passage cited above, Deuteronomy 7:1-2, refers not to killing but to driving out the land's inhabitants.

In other words, many Canaanites left voluntarily when they learned the Israelites were coming. They had heard about how Israel escaped from Egypt through the miraculous parting of the Red Sea and knew they were outgunned (see Joshua 2:9). Others who remained to fight but survived the battle likely fled to live elsewhere. Some of those who left later returned.

In all the conquest of Canaan, Israel only instigated two battles, one against Jericho and the other against Ai. All the other battles were started by their enemies. Reading these conquest accounts as they were intended to be read, in their historical context, explains or explains away a lot of the violence.

That which remains needs to be read in light of the character of the God who commanded it. He is, after all, the sovereign of the universe. He owns all by virtue of having created all. If He determines that a certain territory belongs to His people, then others living there are trespassing. God made no secret of His intention to remove these trespassers and give the land to His people, announcing this several hundred years earlier (see Genesis 15). If Rahab's words to the spies are any indication (see Joshua 2:9-11), God's intentions were clearly understood by the inhabitants of Canaan.

By this time, God had already clearly revealed Himself as merciful. Remember how He provided for Adam and Eve even after they had sinned, how He did the same for Cain, how He warned the wicked in Noah's day, how He warned the Egyptians during the plagues and how He welcomed the Egyptians who chose to join the Israelites. In these instances and others, God went out of His way to avoid bloodshed.

This is why, though He commanded the removal of the Canaanites, God also limited the war against them. Only certain cities were targeted for complete destruction, likely as warnings to the rest. Although Rahab had been targeted for destruction, God welcomed into His community her and her family when they confessed their loyalty. God even expressed concern about the feelings of those captured in battle (see Deuteronomy 21:10-14).

When we read about this violence, we also need to remember God's plan. This plan called for sin's eventual removal through the cross of Jesus. While God was preparing for this moment, sin and its effects remained. God provided ways to help His people cope, but even some of these work-arounds were tainted by sin. Take human government, for example. While government is essential to restraining sin, it can't do so without constraint which sometimes requires violence, whether through policing or warfare.

This was also true for the nation of Israel. It had to practice violence against threats from within and from without. The alternative would have been the disappearance of the nation of Israel. Even the law of Moses does not eliminate violence but teaches the Israelites how to employ it selectively and effectively. To reinforce that lesson, the law displays God as an example of One who perfectly balances justice and mercy.

Further, the law clarifies *why* the Israelites must survive, because they are the source of God's blessing to the rest of the world. The proper exercise of violence in a fallen world was necessary to accomplish God's plan to eliminate violence.

It may be best to see the violence in the Book of Joshua as a kind of surgery. No one criticizes a surgeon for taking a blade and cutting into a living body. Everyone understands that such violence is needed to accomplish a greater good, restoring health. God's commands for violence should be understood this way, as surgery necessary to accomplish the greatest good.

Humanity was diseased and needed healing. That healing involved the choice of Abraham, from whom a nation would come. From that nation would come Jesus, the Healer of all broken relationships. For that nation to flourish, God provided a land where they could learn how to be God's people and spread their influence among other nations.

As we saw above, Canaan was the perfect place for this to happen. Those living in the land needed to be removed in order for Israel to carry out its God-assigned role. The Canaanites were entrenched in pagan idolatry. They may not have been any worse than the Egyptians or Mesopotamians, but they were living on God's land and for that reason needed to be removed. If they remained, God told the Israelites, they would be like "snares and traps for you, whips on your backs and thorns in your eyes, until you perish from this good land, which the LORD your God has given you" (Joshua 23:12-13). For God's plan to succeed, the Canaanites would have to go.

Ultimately, the violence in the Old Testament can only be understood in light of the cross. The cross proves how much God hates violence. He hates it so much He allowed Himself to be crucified, one of the most violent ways ever known to kill someone. God took on violence in this extreme form in order to destroy its power and restore us to harmony with Himself.

Disaster follows disobedience

For the most part, the Book of Joshua illustrates the first part of the principle of retribution, that obedience brings blessing. Because of the obedience shown by Joshua and the Israelites, they took possession of the promised land and were poised to remove the Canaanites who remained.

Sadly, the second part of this principle, that disobedience brings disaster, is abundantly illustrated in the Book of Judges. Things started out well, with Israel gathering to fight against a common foreign enemy, but things do not end well.

When Joshua died, God did not appoint someone to succeed him. Instead, God raised up judges to lead his people. Don't think of robed men and women seated in a courtroom. Old Testament judges were more like a combination of judge, general, and tribal chief ruling over one or more of Israel's tribes.

The judge's number one job was to provide justice for God's people. When injustice came from another Israelite, the judge set up court and made sure the aggrieved got what was due (see Judges 4:4-5). If the injustice came from foreigners, the judge suited up for battle, gathered an army and fought until justice prevailed (see Judges 4:6-10).

A pattern soon developed among the Israelites. As God had warned, they began to be corrupted by the Canaanites who remained or who had returned. God punished the Israelites by allowing foreign nations to oppress them. In the face of this oppression the Israelites called out to God for help. He raised up a judge who brought liberation. When that judge died, however, the Israelites slipped back into their idolatrous pattern and the cycle started all over again (see Judges 2:11-19).

This was not a cycle like a revolving wheel, but more of a downward spiral, with life in Israel becoming worse and worse. While the book begins with Israel asking God who should lead their armies against a foreign enemy, it ends with them asking God who should lead their armies against one of their own tribes. Twice the book's author observes that "everyone did as they saw fit" (see Judges 17:6; 21:25). Anarchy had descended upon Israel.

What they really needed was a strong leader, someone like Moses, Joshua, or a king. But "in those days Israel had no king" (Judges 17:6; 21:25). If this was what they needed, why didn't God provide it right away after Joshua died? Apparently, God wanted His people to experience the consequences of their disobedience. The judges were work-arounds to help Israel avoid the worst of these consequences, while still allowing them to clearly see the great cost of sin and the great need for a righteous monarch.

God would eventually give them a king. We will explore how this happened in the next chapter. But before we do, we must now consider a beautiful little love story that took place during this disastrous period. This story, though small, illustrates an important lesson: even when it seems like God is silent, He isn't.

The power of love

During the time of the judges, a couple lived in Judah with two sons. When famine struck their land, they decided to move to the neighboring country of Moab. There the man died. The two sons married Moabite women, but then the two sons died.

When Naomi, the widowed mother, heard that the famine in Judah had ended, she and her two daughters-in-law began the journey home, hoping for a better life. On the way, Naomi offered her daughters-in-law the chance to remain in their homeland. One accepted the opportunity but the other committed herself to Naomi and to all it meant to be one of God's chosen people. While the Book of Judges describes the Israelites living like foreigners, here is a foreigner who chose to become an Israelite.

The two widows returned to a challenging existence. Without men to support them, they were economically and socially vulnerable. Ruth, the daughter-in-law, worked hard to provide for them by gleaning in the fields of others. This practice of gleaning was a work-around included in the law to provide for the poor. Israelite farmers were commanded to leave a little of their crop at the edges of the fields so the poor could gather enough to eat.

One day, Ruth found herself gleaning in the field of an older man, Boaz, who she later learned was actually a "kinsman redeemer" to Naomi. This was another work-around in the law that provided a built-in support system. It allowed for one relative, the kinsman redeemer, to intervene on behalf of a relative who had fallen on hard times. The redeemer could buy back land that had been sold or help out in other ways.

Boaz recognized his responsibility and not only intervened on behalf of Naomi, but married Ruth. Their child continued the family name of Naomi's dead husband (something very important in that culture). This boy also became the grandfather of David, the future king of Israel, and an ancestor to Jesus.

While the Israelites were proving themselves faithless, a foreigner was proving faithful. God worked through her faithfulness to bring what Israel needed most, a righteous king. How God brought that king to power and established his dynasty is where we turn next as we examine the big picture of the Bible.

Study Questions

1. I've provided several examples from the Book of Joshua how God taught His people to trust Him. Can you find other ways He did so?

2. I suggested that to understand the violence in the Old Testament, we need to read these passages in their historical context and in light of God's character and plan. How might you might explain the violence in the Bible to someone troubled by it?

3. What other examples of the principle of retribution can you find in the books of Joshua, Judges, and Ruth?

4. God allowed the Israelites to experience the period of the Judges in order to help them see the need for something better, a righteous king. Can you think of situations in your own life where God allowed you to experience difficulty to prepare your heart for something better?

Chapter Seven

THE LEADER FOR GOD'S PEOPLE

1 Samuel – 2 Kings

Longing for a king

Through many centuries and lots of messiness, God's plan to restore harmony in His creation has continued to unfold. Meanwhile, God the teacher has been schooling His pupils in important lessons, especially the need to live by faith. God has also graciously set in place work-arounds to help His people navigate their less-than-perfect world.

In the last chapter we saw one of those work-arounds, the succession of judges. God's intent was for His people to be delivered from their oppressors, but also to see the need for a strong leader who could bring together all twelve tribes and lead them as God's representative. He wanted the Israelites to see their need for a king, but one "after God's own heart."

Even before the Israelites entered the land of Canaan, God predicted they would ask for a king (see Deuteronomy 17:14-20). He knew that day would come and, when it did, God didn't reject the idea or blame the Israelites for thinking this way. Instead God provided clear instructions for the kind of person to choose and how he is to govern.

Earlier we noted that the Book of Judges anticipated the day when Israel would be ruled by a king who would replace anarchy with stability. In this chapter we'll see that God not only selected the king He wanted, but made it clear that kingship should continue for years to come.

There are some passages, however, where it looks like God opposed the idea of Israel having a king, only granting it as a concession to their faithlessness (see 1 Samuel 8; 12). Samuel, the godly judge who brought stability and unity to Israel, didn't think a king was such a good idea. He assumed God wanted to continue with judges, appointing his sons to succeed him (see 1 Samuel 8:1).

The people didn't like that option. They knew Samuel's sons were dishonest, so they asked for a king instead (see 1 Samuel 8:5). Samuel was unhappy about this request, as was God who speaks of the people as rejecting not just Samuel but Himself (see 1 Samuel 8:7).

To be clear, God doesn't object to the Israelites having a king, but to Israel's motive in asking for one. They want a king for the security, prosperity and prestige they think the king could bring them. They don't realize that a king's most important quality should not be physical prowess, military expertise, political acumen, or leadership skills. What a king needs most is a heart that values what God values, a heart patterned after God's heart. They need a king like God.

The picture of God as king is found throughout the Bible, but we often misunderstand it. We tend to think of a king like the English and European monarchs we learned about in high school. We imagine God as a super-sized version of Henry VIII, a despot who demands absolute obedience or else . . . well, just ask Henry's many wives.

This isn't an accurate picture of an ancient Near Eastern king, let alone God. Yes, some could be quite despotic and ruthless, but the standard job description of a king called for someone much more humane. He was to be someone his subjects should obey and support, but he was also responsible to look after and provide for his people, especially the weakest of his people.

When it comes to God as king, a much better model than Henry VIII would be an African tribal chief. Those within a particular tribe must listen to their chief and do what he says. I was traveling in Africa with a young man from a tribe in Zambia. He mentioned he was moving from one city to another because his chief had told him to. I tried to hide my surprise, thinking how a typical North American young adult would have responded.

Along with that authority over his people, however, is a strong commitment by the chief to do what is best for his tribe. If a widow in the tribe needs a new hut, the chief is responsible for marshalling the tribe's resources to build it. The welfare of the tribe ultimately rests on his shoulders.

When God described Himself as king of Israel, this, not Henry VIII, was what He had in mind. God would be their king, taking responsibility for their well-being, their *shalom*, their peace. They would be His people, unflinching in their loyalty to Him and fully obedient to His commands; they would "love" Him with their whole heart, soul, and strength (see Deuteronomy 6:5).

Israel's king was to be the human representative of the heavenly king. The people would be loyal to him and he would look after them. He was to rule with authority, but as one under God's authority, obedient to His law. He would be judged on how well he looked after God's interest and those of God's people.

Kingship was a work-around. God used this form of government to foster a stable society in which people could experience peace, contentment and prosperity; in other words, it was a system designed to foster a measure of harmony with God, with each other, with self, and with the natural world. Kingship was one of the ways God sought to help people cope with life in a fallen universe.

God chose this form of government for Israel, not because He prefers a monarchy to other possibilities, but because at that time most nations had monarchies. God works with people where they are. He wanted Israel to understand that power is meant to enable service, that true leadership requires sacrifice, and that the greatest leader is the one who leads others in service to God.

Saul: a promising failure

This picture of the ideal monarch was far from the mind of the Israelites as they stood before Samuel that day. They wanted to have a king "such as all the other nations have" (1 Samuel 8:5). Most especially, they wanted someone who could bring them victory over the Philistines, a stronger and more technologically advanced nation living next door (see 1 Samuel 13:19-22).

For this assignment, Saul seemed the perfect candidate. He was handsome and tall, standing "a head taller than anyone else" (1 Samuel 9:2). Then as now, tall stature was considered an asset in leadership. He was also brave, even willing to lead Israel against a superior foe (see 1 Samuel 11).

Saul was humble. He was so reluctant to assume this role he hid among the supplies when the selection was made (see 1 Samuel 10:21-22). At least early on he even seems to have been especially pious, pardoning his detractors and readily acknowledging God as the source of victory (see 1 Samuel 11:13).

But the pressures of kingship revealed the weakness in Saul's character. He lacked the resolve to obey God. Sometimes he failed to do what God had commanded (see 1 Samuel 13:1-14; 1 Samuel 15:1-9). At other times he was overly zealous, going beyond God's direction (see 1 Samuel 14:24; 2 Samuel 21:1-2). He became proud, setting up a monument "in his own honor" (1 Samuel 15:12). His later years reveal a tragic figure, so far from following God's agenda that he seeks to kill the man God had appointed to succeed him.

Sometimes God grants our requests to help us understand what we should have asked for in the first place. That is what happened with the Israelites and Saul. God permitted Saul's reign to show the Israelites the importance of appointing the right person to be king. He gave them what they wanted, even though it was the wrong king, to help them recognize the right one. After all, they weren't just any nation, they had been chosen to bless all other nations. For this, they needed the right kind of king, one whose priorities were the same as Yahweh's.

Keep your eyes on the Ark

The author of the books of First and Second Samuel has given us an indicator of Israel's spiritual health, the Ark of the Covenant. This was a piece of furniture that was located in the innermost room in the sacred Tabernacle. As this tent was understood to be God's palace, and the inner sanctum, God's throne room, the Ark was seen to represent God's throne.

Usually the Ark remained inside the Tabernacle, but was occasionally brought out for various reasons, such as to seek God's will (see Joshua 7:6 or Judges 20:27) or for special occasions (see Joshua 8:33). It was also used in battle to signify God's presence, as when the Israelites carried it across the Jordan (see Joshua 3) or when marching around Jericho (see Joshua 6).

So, when the priests carried the Ark into battle against the Philistines in 1 Samuel 4, they anticipated great victory. Instead, we witness a terrible defeat, with the Ark captured by the enemy (see 1 Samuel 4:11). Israel's religious leaders had become so totally corrupt, even the Ark of the Covenant could not protect them from their punishment.

While in captivity, the Ark remained a powerful weapon, creating destruction and fear among its captors (see 1 Samuel 5). The Israelites had been defeated, but not God. The Philistines became so frightened of the Ark and the God it represented, they eagerly returned it to the Israelites (see 1 Samuel 6).

Saul showed little interest in the Ark. We know he consulted it for guidance on one occasion, although he didn't even give God a chance to answer before making up his own mind (see 1 Samuel 14:18-19). During Saul's reign, the ark remained on the margins of Israel's society. This would change when David became king, a signal that here was a king who genuinely desired God's presence.

David, a man after God's heart

The choice of David as Israel's next king marks a significant step forward in God's plan to bring reconciliation to the world through Israel. God had already provided this nation with a law and a land. Now He would give them their greatest leader.

David and his son, Solomon, presided over Israel's golden age. Never before or since would the twelve tribes be so unified nor would the kingdom be as strong or expansive. At no other time in its existence did the Israelites ever come closer to harmony with God and in all other relationships.

This golden age saw the construction of the temple. The temple was more than just the next logical step in worship structures. Having reached the promised land they could now retire the tabernacle that had been designed for a people on the move.

The temple represented a grand statement of permanence, prominence, and presence; Israel and its God were here to stay and to stay together. Although only a work-around, the temple would become a powerful symbol of God's presence for hundreds of years until destroyed by the Babylonians. It would retain its imprint on the psyche of Israel long after the building lay in ruins.

The golden age of Israel was also the season when Israel's worship underwent a significant upgrade. The essential patterns of priesthood, sacrifice, ritual, and festival continued as described in the law of Moses. But these were enriched with music, songs, and other elaborations. Many of the psalms were written during this time.

As a story, the life of David ranks among the greatest sagas in literature. His rise from tending his father's flock to shepherding God's people has captivated the imagination for millennia.

As a story within God's big story, the life of David is even more significant. David's rule became the standard against which all other kings were measured. So great was David's rule that he came to embody Israel's hope for a glorious future: a great king in the line of David. God had promised David a dynasty; one of his sons would always rule God's people. This promise fueled Israel's anticipation for one of David's descendants to become the Messiah, the Anointed One.

David's long and exciting life, from his selection by Samuel to his death-bed instructions to Solomon, reveals the imprint of God's hand. He recognized something in David and sought to develop it, for David's good, for the good of those he ruled, and as an example to others. God saw that David was a man "after God's heart."

This or a similar description of David is found in 1 Samuel 13:14 and Acts 13:22. It is not meant to suggest that he was perfect and never made mistakes. He did, some of them very serious. Nor is the phrase "after God's heart" primarily meant to suggest that David chased after or pursued God, desirous of fellowship with Him. David did pursue God, but the expression means more.

To be "after God's heart" refers primarily to David's priorities. What mattered to God mattered to David. He cared more about what God cared about than he cared about himself. For this reason, David grieved deeply when he stumbled and quickly repented. David's priorities prompted him to pursue God, for his heart was patterned after God's heart.

Because David understood that God's chief desire was to be in fellowship with His people in worship, David made God's presence a priority. His first official action as king was to return the Ark of the Covenant to Jerusalem, David's capital. He knew instinctively that God belonged at the center of things (see 2 Samuel 6).

The king's great longing in life was to build a temple for God. Even when God refused David this opportunity and assigned the task to Solomon, David actively worked to prepare for the building. He stockpiled great quantities of material, laid out a design, and enriched the musical worship. David cared about what mattered to God, especially that God's people would worship in His presence.

After David's death, Solomon built the temple his father had planned. A glorious building, dazzling with gold, it stood as a tangible indication of how much God's presence mattered to David and his son. In solemn assembly, the Ark of the Covenant, which had languished on the margins in Saul's day and was brought closer to the center of Israel's life in David's, is finally brought to rest where it belonged, in the Most Holy Place. God is at home, in the center of His people. He shows His approval by filling the new temple with a cloud, signifying His glorious presence (see 1 Kings 8:1-11).

Although his heart beat with God's, David still had many important lessons to learn in order to become the king God intended. You won't be surprised to hear that among the most important was the need for faith. He learned this lesson well, employing great faith early in his battle with Goliath (see 1 Samuel 17).

He learned first-hand the important lesson that God can use anyone to do great things. Even a shepherd boy could become Israel's greatest king. Like Abraham, Jacob, Joseph and others before him, David learned that while we tend to judge by outward appearance, God "looks at the heart" (1 Samuel 16:7).

Although anointed Israel's next king when only a boy, David had to wait many years before the crown was placed on his head. In the meantime, King Saul sought to remove that head, chasing him around the wilderness. During those years, David must have been tempted to give up on his calling. We know he had opportunities to kill Saul and take the throne by force. Instead he patiently waited, confident in God's promises. Because David was a man "after God's heart," he learned his lessons well.

The divided monarchy

Sadly, Israel's golden age lasted only about a century before serious troubles developed. Blessings followed obedience, but the disobedience of the kings, beginning with Solomon, led to great disaster.

After Solomon's death, his kingdom split into two, one containing primarily the tribe of Judah, the other made up of the ten northern tribes. The latter took the name, Israel, and eventually established its capital in Samaria. The former took the name of Judah, with its capital in Jerusalem.

The northern kingdom, Israel, began with a serious political problem, the temple was located in another country. A new sanctuary would need to be created or else the people's loyalty would be divided. The northern kingdom's first king, Jeroboam, established two sanctuaries, one near his southern border and one in the north. He also established calf idols at these sanctuaries and set up his own systems for worship, rather than those of God's design (see 1 Kings 12:26-33).

Once set on this trajectory of disobedience, the history of the northern kingdom was marked by one disaster after another. No single dynasty lasted very long; each new dynasty began with bloodshed and warfare. After a little more than 200 years, the northern kingdom fell to the Assyrian Empire. Many of its people were uprooted and scattered around the Near East, eventually being absorbed and obliterated. Hence the ten lost tribes of Israel.

The southern kingdom, Judah, lasted 136 years longer. They had about the same number of kings as their northern neighbors, but the southern kings reigned longer on average, and all came from the same Davidic dynasty.

Of the thirty-nine kings who ruled in both kingdoms after Solomon, eight were identified as doing what God approved, as David had done (see 1 Kings 15:11). All eight were from the southern kingdom and each one showed particular care for what mattered to God. Obedience brought blessing.

Even the southern kingdom eventually succumbed to the disobedience of its kings and people. It was captured by the Babylonians in 586 BC, with Jerusalem and the temple suffering destruction and the population taken into exile. But unlike the Assyrians, the Babylonian policy was to allow the Judeans to settle together in groups. As such, they retained their identity as God's people during the half century they spent in exile.

Hope out of disaster

Looked at from one angle, the monarchy had been a total disaster. First the division of one kingdom into rivals, then the total defeat of both due to disobedience, the loss of the temple and finally exile from the land promised to Abraham. God's plan to establish a nation had come to nothing. With the end of the nation came the end of God's redemptive plan, or so it would appear.

Looked at from another angle, God was working, even through disaster. As we have seen Him do many times by now, God redeemed the worst. He used these disasters and the time in exile to largely purge the Israelites of their tendency toward idolatry and create within them a thirst for God's law. They returned much more inclined to listen to God.

He brought good things out of the monarchy. It formed in Israel's collective mind a picture of the perfect king, a future Son of David who would restore the kingdom. Later Israelites looked back to this picture with hope for a better day.

During the worst of the monarchy, God sent prophets to call His people back to obedience. The ministry of the prophets not only laid out more clearly what it meant to obey, but revealed more fully the blessings that would result. Their pictures of a future hope, including complete reconciliation, inspired Israel for centuries to come. We will look more closely at the prophets in a future chapter.

God also used the period of the monarchy to dig a deep well of piety and wisdom. Books like Psalms and Proverbs were largely composed during these years. Their insights encouraged the Israelites returning from exile to rebuild their lives and work toward the fulfillment of God's plan. We turn now to draw from this deep well.

Study Questions

1. God allowed the Israelites to experience Saul to prepare them for David. In what ways have you seen God permit in your life what He doesn't prefer, to prepare you for what is better?

2. David's sin with Bathsheba produced long-lasting effects. Why doesn't God, along with forgiving our sins, also eliminate their effects?

3. The northern kingdom experienced the illusion of success (things like prosperity and security), even as it was a total failure because of idolatry. How can we distinguish between what is true success and what is only illusory?

4. Does the principle of retribution still apply today?

Chapter Eight

<u>DEEP WELL</u>

Proverbs, Job, Ecclesiastes, Song of Songs, Psalms

What is wisdom literature?

Up to this point we've looked at how God's redemptive plan developed over time. This chapter takes a different approach, pausing at one period, the monarchy, to see how God's plan was expressed in Israel's literature. In particular, we'll explore the literature they used in their worship and the literature through which they taught wisdom.

Let's begin with wisdom literature. Probably all cultures have something like this, writings designed to help people live well. Works like Aesop's Fables from early Greece and Poor Richard's Almanac from early America are two examples.

Wisdom literature can be found among Israel's neighbors as well. Much of it dealt with common themes, such as how to succeed in life and how to deal with suffering and disappointment.

This apparently universal practice of collecting and dispensing time-honored wisdom is one of God's work-arounds. He understood that people would need help living in a fallen world, particularly how to avoid common problems and find happiness.

Seeing the wisdom tradition as God's idea helps explain why so much of the wisdom is similar, even though it comes from different countries. It is as if God stored such insights in aquifers, underground lakes from which a variety of people drew up through the well of their own cultures.

The uniqueness of Israel's wisdom, whether found in Proverbs, Job, Ecclesiastes, or Song of Songs, is not in its literary style; similar examples for each of these books can be found among Israel's neighbors. Nor is Israel's wisdom unique because of how it was learned. God didn't deliver this wisdom from above, as He gave the law on Mt. Sinai, but from below, from everyday life.

Israel's wisdom literature is unique for at least two reasons. First, Israel knew best who put the aquifer there in the first place: Yahweh, their God. Everyone in the ancient Near East believed that true wisdom came from the gods; Israel knew who that true God was; they knew the true source of wisdom.

This allowed them to recognize Yahweh's wisdom in all things, in nature, the human heart, inter-personal interaction, and humanity's relationship with God. There was no such thing as secular wisdom; all wisdom was God's. Here again, Israel was not unique in seeing the pervasiveness of divinely given wisdom. But they understood that only one God had created everything, and that God was Yahweh, who had chosen them as His people.

Second, Israel's wisdom identifies life's ultimate goal as something greater than knowledge and success. We were made to have reverence for God. Here again, other nations saw wisdom as living in step with the supernatural, but Israel understood the supernatural better than her neighbors. Hence, God's people knew better what it meant to fear God.

The fear of God is the most important concept in all of Israel's wisdom literature. The opening of the Book of Proverbs uses this concept to describe how to become wise (see Proverbs 1:7). We find the fear of God at the middle of the Book of Job as the secret to dealing with suffering (see Job 28:28). After the Teacher's long search in Ecclesiastes, he concludes that the fear of God is the best way to handle deep discouragement (see Ecclesiastes 12:13).

Fear of Yahweh (or God, or the Lord) doesn't mean being afraid of God. It involves reverence in relationship. To fear God doesn't mean we're too afraid to approach Him, but that we come near with reverence. We recognize that He is perfect and we are sinful, He is strong and we are weak, He knows all and we are uninformed, He is God and we aren't.

But the key is reverence in relationship. We may not be God, but God has invited us to have fellowship with Him. The perfect God has made it possible for us to enter His presence. The strong and wise God has offered to share His strength and wisdom with us. More than any other nation, Israel understood the true nature of this relationship, having been made God's covenant partners.

This gave rise to one of Israel's most delightful and distinctive qualities, covenant confidence. It was this that allowed Abraham to question God about the absence of the promised heir (see Genesis 15). It was covenant confidence by which he negotiated with God to spare Sodom (see Genesis 18). We see this confidence in Joseph who was able to forgive his brothers for selling him into slavery, knowing that God had used their treachery for good (see Genesis 50:20).

We see this confidence in King David who humbly acknowledged that he owes God everything, but then reminded God to keep His promise to establish David's dynasty (see 2 Samuel 7, especially verse 25-26). We see this covenant confidence many times in the psalms. Because Israel understood the fear of the LORD, they were both reverent and bold.

We've noticed several times that God instructs His people like a teacher instructs his students, usually on the topic of faith. Fear of the Lord is just another way of describing faith. Because Abraham revered God he trusted Him enough to leave his homeland at God's command. Because he revered God he believed God could provide a son in his old age and because he and God were in relationship, he believed God would do just that.

A work-around for living sensibly

Not only do the wisdom books teach the importance of faith, they also show how to experience some degree of reconciliation in one's relationships. Let's begin with the Book of Proverbs. It contains brief, often two-line aphorisms, that dispense the wisdom of living sensibly.

Some of these proverbs address the benefits of living in fellowship with God. Such as:

> The LORD does not let the righteous go hungry,
> but he thwarts the craving of the wicked (Proverbs 10:3).

> The fear of the LORD adds length to life,
> but the years of the wicked are cut short.
> The prospect of the righteous is joy,
> but the hopes of the wicked come to nothing.
> The way of the LORD is a refuge for the blameless,
> but it is the ruin of those who do evil.
> The righteous will never be uprooted,
> but the wicked will not remain in the land (Proverbs 10:27-30).

> Better the poor whose walk is blameless
> than a fool whose lips are perverse (Proverbs 19:1).

> To do what is right and just
> is more acceptable to the LORD than sacrifice.
> Haughty eyes and a proud heart
> —the unplowed field of the wicked—
> produce sin (Proverbs 21:3-4)

Even when they don't do so explicitly, all the proverbs imply the importance of this primary relationship. Most concern how wisdom impacts the other three relationships.

The Book of Proverbs provides practical advice about how to live successfully amidst a fallen natural world. For example:

> Put your outdoor work in order
> and get your fields ready;
> after that, build your house (Proverbs 24:27).

> I went past the field of a sluggard,
> past the vineyard of someone who has no sense;
> thorns had come up everywhere,
> the ground was covered with weeds,
> and the stone wall was in ruins.
> I applied my heart to what I observed
> and learned a lesson from what I saw:
> A little sleep, a little slumber,
> a little folding of the hands to rest—
> and poverty will come on you like a thief
> and scarcity like an armed man (Proverbs 24:30-34).

> Whoever loves pleasure will become poor;
> whoever loves wine and olive oil will never be rich
> (Proverbs 21:17).

> The righteous care for the needs of their animals,
> but the kindest acts of the wicked are cruel (Proverbs 12:10).

Several proverbs help us find reconciliation with self, such as:

> A happy heart makes the face cheerful,
> but heartache crushes the spirit (Proverbs 15:13).

> A cheerful heart is good medicine,
> but a crushed spirit dries up the bones (Proverbs 17:22).

> Better to be lowly in spirit along with the oppressed
> than to share plunder with the proud (Proverbs 16:19).

The human spirit can endure in sickness,
but a crushed spirit who can bear? (Proverbs 18:14).

The human spirit is the lamp of the LORD
that sheds light on one's inmost being (Proverbs 20:27).

Deceit is in the hearts of those who plot evil,
but those who promote peace have joy (Proverbs 12:20).

Each heart knows its own bitterness,
and no one else can share its joy (Proverbs 14:10).

We also find many proverbs explaining how to experience interpersonal harmony. Here are several examples:

Better to live on a corner of the roof
than share a house with a quarrelsome wife (Proverbs 21:9).

A gentle answer turns away wrath,
but a harsh word stirs up anger (Proverbs 15:1).

A hot-tempered person stirs up conflict,
but the one who is patient calms a quarrel (Proverbs 15:18).

A prudent servant will rule over a disgraceful son
and will share the inheritance as one of the family
(Proverbs 17:2).

Whoever would foster love covers over an offense,
but whoever repeats the matter separates close friends
(Proverbs 17:9).

A person's wisdom yields patience;
it is to one's glory to overlook an offense (Proverbs 19:11).

Discipline your children, for in that there is hope;
do not be a willing party to their death.

A hot-tempered person must pay the penalty;
rescue them, and you will have to do it again
(Proverbs 19:18-19).

Do not eat the food of a begrudging host,
do not crave his delicacies;
for he is the kind of person
who is always thinking about the cost.
"Eat and drink," he says to you,
but his heart is not with you.
You will vomit up the little you have eaten
and will have wasted your compliments (Proverbs 23:6-8).

A work-around for suffering

Although very different in style and subject matter, the Book of Job, like the Book of Proverbs, also provides divine help for living in a fallen world. Specifically, the Book of Job helps us navigate the suffering everyone experiences in such a world.

Suffering is a symptom of our alienation from a fallen natural world that produces sickness and disease. Inter-personal alienation increases as people tend to avoid those who are suffering and as sufferers tend to isolate themselves. Avoidance and self-isolation worsen intra-personal alienation.

What do we learn from this book about how to face suffering? Since Job is righteous and yet suffers, we learn that suffering may come to anyone. Job doesn't understand why this is happening to him. His friends try to explain it away, but their explanations seem to make things more confusing. We get a hint in the middle of the book that suffering is best endured in the fear of the Lord (Job 28:28).

What had been only a hint bursts into full view in the closing chapters of the book as God personally confronts Job. He doesn't come to answer Job's questions, but to ask a few of His own. God's questions show that He remains in control of the natural world even though suffering makes it seem otherwise.

God's questions are rhetorical; they confront Job's lack of understanding, not to belittle him, but to highlight how much wiser God must be. God comforts Job, as G. K. Chesterton put it, with paradoxes. Pain makes us doubt, but we must continue to doubt until we doubt our own capacity to solve our problem by our understanding. We must learn to walk by faith, not by sight.

This comforting confrontation would likely not have happened without Job's covenant confidence. He appealed to God to hear his complaint and trusted in God's care (Job 13:18; 23:3-5; 19:25). Although God scolds Job for claiming to know more than he actually did, He still pays him a high compliment when He says twice that Job understood God better than his friends did (see Job 42:7-8).

How do we live in a world that leaves us susceptible to suffering? Like Job, we respond in covenant confidence. Through reverence in relationship we can find peace in our pain.

A work-around for despair

The Book of Ecclesiastes tackles a different symptom of a fallen world, the feeling that life has no meaning. This is one of the most debilitating forms of intra-personal alienation, since it blocks out any ray of hope.

This book describes the search for meaning in all the usual places: wisdom, pleasure, wealth, beauty, accomplishment. But no matter where "The Teacher" turns, all is meaningless. Between the lines of his advice on how to cope with this feeling is the gnawing sense that even "The Teacher" hasn't found what he's looking for.

I wish I could say that this book ends on a bright note, with "The Teacher" having a good heart-to-heart talk with God. It doesn't. It's a pretty depressing book, but for some, life is like that. For all of us, but especially for these, we need to hear that when you can't seem to make sense of anything, when you're discouraged and hopeless, when you've become cynical, you can still do something: "Fear God and keep his commandments, for this is the duty of all mankind" (Ecclesiastes 12:13).

I love how the work-around of wisdom works in any weather. Whether you're having a "Proverbs" day and need to know how to make the most out of life, or a "Job" day, living in pain and confusion, or an "Ecclesiastes" day when getting out of bed is a major accomplishment, wisdom can help. Even in a fallen world, reverence in relationship can bring a measure of harmony with Him, with others, with yourself, and with your world.

Marriage: One of God's best work-arounds

Before turning to the Book of Psalms, we need to say a word about a little book, often neglected, but filled with insights into complete reconciliation. This book, Song of Songs (or Song of Solomon), is filled with ancient Near East love poetry, not unlike what we find in Egypt from around this same time.

Through poetry, the book tells the story of the love between a man and a woman. We observe their mutual respect; there is no hierarchy here, only mutual strength and mutual weakness. The language is metaphorical, but we have no trouble recognizing beautiful, exclusive, joy-filled intimacy between the couple.

As we read, it dawns on us that this book is describing one of God's greatest work-arounds, marriage. In marriage, we unite with another person in a way that can do more to bring inter-personal and intra-personal harmony than any other relationship can do.

Marriage can also bring a measure of healing to our relationship with the natural world. Not only can two live more cheaply than one, research suggests that marriage strengthens our capacity to work and sharpens our motive for doing so. Having spent the past 30 years around college students, I've witnessed the miracle of a less-than-motivated student being transformed into a responsible adult by the experience of marriage.

Marriage can do something even more important. It can help restore our relationship with God. This has long been recognized in many traditions within Christianity. Roman Catholicism views marriage as a sacrament, a means whereby God brings grace into our lives.

In marriage, as in no other human relationship, we have the opportunity to learn the virtues of humility, perseverance, and love. Learning to be humble, to stick at something even when it is hard, and to love in self-sacrificing ways will not only pay dividends in our relationships with our spouse and ourselves, but also with God.

God's wisdom

We have been describing how wisdom literature provides many work-arounds for living in a fallen world. They do something more. They actually anticipate the day when work-arounds are no longer needed.

Almost from the time it was written, Song of Songs was understood to refer, not only to human love between a man and a woman, but to the love between God and humanity. Marriage not only brings us closer to God, it represents that relationship. In this way, it anticipates full reconciliation.

The Book of Job not only offers guidance for how to live wisely while suffering, it anticipates the day when suffering will end.

The Old Testament contains only a handful of references to bodily resurrection; several are found in the Book of Job (see Job 19:26). The recognition that suffering is transformed by the presence of God helps us anticipate our heavenly reward when there will be no more "mourning or crying or pain" (Revelation 21:4).

In addition to its helpful counsel on how to live in a fallen world, the Book of Proverbs also anticipates a world no longer tainted by sin. In Proverbs 8, Wisdom personified speaks in the first person, describing her presence at the beginning and her involvement in creation. Later Jewish and Christian writers will develop further this idea of Wisdom serving as an intermediary between humanity and God (for example, see 1 Corinthians 1:21-30; Colossians 2:3).

Psalms to worship the King

The Book of Psalms is a collection of songs used in the Temple to worship Yahweh. The collection spans several hundred years and various types of songs and is actually a collection of collections. King David's name is associated with about half of the psalms, although we aren't sure whether as author, collector, subject, commissioner, or something else.

One thing all 150 psalms have in common is that all are a form of praise. The name of this book in Hebrew is "Book of Praises." They don't all sound like praises, especially the psalms that complain to God, but that has more to do with our deficient understanding of praise than with the psalms themselves.

The psalms also share a common theme: God's rule as King. Remember we're talking about a king more like an African tribal chief than Henry VIII. God holds absolute power but has committed Himself to the well-being of His subjects, particularly Israel. God provided the Book of Psalms so His people could better understand what it meant for Him to be their King and they His subjects.

Many of the psalms praise God directly for His reign and its benefits (see Psalm 103, 23). He rules all nations, but has chosen Israel to be His special possession, as we see from Psalm 47:

> [1] Clap your hands, all you nations;
>   shout to God with cries of joy.
>
> [2] For the LORD Most High is awesome,
>   the great King over all the earth.
>
> [3] He subdued nations under us,
>   peoples under our feet.
>
> [4] He chose our inheritance for us,
>   the pride of Jacob, whom he loved.
>
> [5] God has ascended amid shouts of joy,
>   the LORD amid the sounding of trumpets.
>
> [6] Sing praises to God, sing praises;
>   sing praises to our King, sing praises.
>
> [7] For God is the King of all the earth;
>   sing to him a psalm of praise.
>
> [8] God reigns over the nations;
>   God is seated on his holy throne.
>
> [9] The nobles of the nations assemble
>   as the people of the God of Abraham,
>   for the kings of the earth belong to God;
>   he is greatly exalted.

Others psalms praise God indirectly by praising some aspect of His rule. For example, they might praise the earthly king (see Psalm 45), or the law (see Psalm 1, 119), or Jerusalem (see Psalm 46, 87), or the temple (see Psalm 48).

These become praises to God because of their connection with God. He chose the earthly king, gave the law, selected Jerusalem, and inhabits His temple. Their chief value and the reason we celebrate them is their association with God the King.

Other psalms take a very different tone, complaining to God. While we don't normally consider this an act of praise, Israel did. They knew that as their King, God was responsible for helping when things weren't happening as He promised they would. Rather than taking matters into their own hands, they took their problems to God. They praise God by assuming He will intercede on their behalf based on their covenant confidence as His subjects.

A work-around through worship

God provided the Book of Psalms as part of His curriculum, in order to help the Israelites understand what it meant to be the people of God. He also gave the psalms as a work-around. Using these psalms in worship, God allowed His people to experience a measure of reconciliation.

God inspired these words so that Israel could voice their praises to Him. These psalms teach us about God, but they are more than lessons. They are vehicles that usher us into God's presence in worship. They provide us the script for worship. Our greatest problem is our separation from God; God meets our need with psalms that usher us into His presence and give us the words to say when we get there.

When in His presence we find we can be completely honest and open. True praise allows us to bring our deepest thoughts—even our complaints—to the only One who can help us. Worship allows us to see the world correctly. Seeing things in light of God's Word corrects our misperceptions.

The Book of Psalms was Israel's songbook. God gave it to help them worship, knowing that worship allows us to experience harmony in our relationship with God, leading to harmony in all our other relationships.

Wisdom, marriage, a script for worship . . . God provided these wonderful gifts to help His people experience some measure of reconciliation in their relationships. Sometimes, however, we need something more direct, like a fearless figure courageously calling out God's people. We need a prophet.

Study Questions

1. How would you help an unbeliever understand why a good and all-powerful God allows suffering?

2. What does the fear of Yahweh—reverence in relationship—look like today?

3. In what ways is marriage a work-around which helps restore all four broken relationships?

4. How can all the psalms, even the ones which express complaints, be a form of praise?

5. Which is your favorite psalm? Why?

Chapter Nine
MY SERVANTS, THE PROPHETS
Isaiah, Jeremiah, Ezekiel, Daniel, and the Minor Prophets

What is a prophet?

Throughout Israel's history, prophets played a role in God's work among His people. In the early days, the roles of leader and prophet were combined, as with Moses (see Deuteronomy 34:10) and Deborah (see Judges 4-5). When the monarchy was young, prophets served as advisors to the king. Think of Nathan conveying God's promise of a dynasty to David (see 2 Samuel 7) or condemning his behavior with Bathsheba (see 2 Samuel 12).

Later in the monarchy, starting midway through the eighth century, we see men and women addressing God's people about the social and spiritual conditions in the kingdoms. Many of these prophets left behind a written record of their messages. We refer to these writing prophets as either Major or Minor; the difference is not the gravity of what they said, but how much of it was preserved.

A prophet was a person called by God to be His spokesperson. The prophet didn't choose this role but was chosen for it. Isaiah 6 records Isaiah's dramatic call. The prophecies of Jeremiah begin with God announcing to this young man that God had set him apart for this role (see Jeremiah 1:5). We see something similar in the opening chapters of Ezekiel. Prophets are called to this role as spokespersons.

By spokesperson, I mean something like a combination of press secretary and ambassador. A press secretary announces, not their own opinion, but that of the official they represent. Just so, the prophet was to announce the message he or she had heard from God. If they said anything more or less, they had failed as a prophet.

They did more than announce the message, they embodied it, like ambassadors. An ambassador is sent to live in another country. There this person communicates messages from the homeland, but also represents the homeland. This helps explain why the prophets often acted out their messages, such as when Hosea was required to marry an adulterous woman (see Hosea 1-3), when Isaiah went around seriously underdressed (see Isaiah 20), or when Ezekiel created a small model of Jerusalem (see Ezekiel 4:1).

"My servants, the prophets"

The prophets were God's "servants" (2 Kings 9:7; Jeremiah 7:25; 26:5; 35:15; 44:4; Ezekiel 38:17) to guide His people in troubled times. The nations of Israel and Judah were experiencing internal and external threats. They needed to know what God thought of their actions and what the consequences would be should those actions continue.

Many people today misread the prophets, thinking of them as primarily predictors of the future. Yes, the prophets made predictions, but their goal was not to tell the future. They primarily announced God's opinion of their present. As someone has put it, the prophets' role was not so much to foretell as to "forth-tell."

The prophets were sent to remind God's people of the terms of the covenant. The Israelites had agreed to live by those terms: to love God completely and love their neighbors as themselves (see Deuteronomy 6:5; Leviticus 19:18). When the people ceased to abide by these terms, God sent the prophets to persuade them to repent and return.

As forth-tellers and covenant enforcers, the prophets represent yet another of God's work-arounds. They were a temporary measure, a way for God to get His message directly to the people, calling them back into a right relationship with Him while His divine plan progressed.

Prophets: tutors of God's people

The prophets sought to persuade God's people to obey the covenant so Israel could fulfill the goal of the covenant. In Genesis 12:1-3, God had tasked Abraham's descendants with becoming a source of blessing to all nations. Through Isaiah He assured them that this remains their mission: "It is too small a thing for you to be my servant to restore the tribes of Jacob and bring back those of Israel I have kept. I will also make you a light for the Gentiles, that my salvation may reach to the ends of the earth" (Isaiah 49:6).

Jeremiah, speaking for God, called the Israelites back to the covenant and their true purpose in these words:

> "If you, Israel, will return, then return to me," declares the LORD. "If you put your detestable idols out of my sight and no longer go astray, and if in a truthful, just and righteous way you swear, 'As surely as the LORD lives,' then the nations will invoke blessings by him and in him they will boast" (Jeremiah 4:1-2).

These words of Jeremiah not only remind us of Abraham's call ("the nations will invoke blessings by him"), they also identify God's two chief complaints against His people. God used the prophets to condemn *idolatry* ("put your detestable idols out of my sight and no longer go astray") and *oppression* ("in a truthful, just and righteous way you swear, 'As surely as the LORD lives'").

Idolatry had always been a great temptation to the Israelites.

Even before Moses descended Mount Sinai, they had created an idol—a golden calf—to worship (see Exodus 32). God warned them sternly against making and worshiping idols in the Ten Commandments (see Exodus 20:3-5) and punished them repeatedly when they disobeyed.

God knows idolatry is something very serious for it represents a betrayal of loyalty. They were to love God with all their heart and this meant absolute loyalty. No wonder God so often compared idolatry to adultery (see Hosea 1-3).

Idolatry degrades God's nature by confining it to some visible form of an animal or person. For an infinite God to be restricted to a visible object means something has been left out. God's people would end up worshiping something less than God and become less than what He envisioned for His people. We always become like what we worship.

Idolatry also represents a step backward from the high level of faith by which He expects His people to live. From the beginning of God's work with His people we have seen the priority He places on walking by faith, not by sight. The Israelites could not please God and fulfill their appointed role except through faith.

While we can and should be critical of Israel's tendency toward idolatry, we should also try to understand the challenge they were up against. They stood alone among their neighbors as the only image-free religion. They also had to resist the very human tendency to represent something invisible by something visible. While it isn't (necessarily) idolatry, think how natural it is for humans to represent the intangible with something tangible, like a nation with a flag, and a sports team with a jersey.

To make things more difficult, God had located them on a busy thoroughfare with people from many different countries traveling north or south. This required Israel to engage in lots of commerce with foreign nations. It also meant they formed alliances for trade and security. All such interactions exposed Israel to the temptation of adopting the images worshiped by other nations. It made good political and economic sense to welcome such gods along with their worshippers. While it made sense in these ways, it made disastrous spiritual sense.

The other category of sin most often challenged by the prophets was oppression, whether involving another nation oppressing Israel, or one Israelite oppressing another Israelite. As we'll see shortly, the prophets had some harsh things to say to foreign oppressors. They were also very critical of the kind of oppression that took place in the markets and courts of Israel, Israelite oppressing Israelite.

In the marketplace, corrupt business practices defrauded the unsuspecting. This might be by dishonest weights and measures (see Micah 6:9-11) or by selling an inferior product as if of high quality (see Amos 8:6). Even worse, they were stealing and extorting from their fellow Israelites (see Habakkuk 2:6).

Some Israelites were conducting business in such a way that the poor became poorer and the rich grew richer. When fellow Israelites became too poor to repay their loans, they were sold into slavery for as little as the price of a pair of sandals (Amos 2:6).

Oppression also occurred in the courts. This is what is meant in Jeremiah 4:2 by swearing falsely. The guilty were swearing their innocence in God's name. When those wronged came for justice, bribery blinded the eyes of the judges. People were literally getting away with murder (see Isaiah 5:7-8; Ezekiel 9:9; Hosea 4:2; Micah 3:9-12).

The two sins, idolatry and oppression, are connected. Both are condemned in the law as out of bounds for God's people. They are connected in another way. Once you become disloyal to

God, you are more likely to mistreat others for your own gain. Alienation from God makes alienation from others more likely.

As we noted above, the prophets not only delivered messages to God's people, but also to Israel's neighbors. Some of these messages were actually communicated to foreigners (see Jeremiah 27; 51:59-64); others were not; all conveyed important truths to Israel. First, they reminded God's people of their covenant responsibility to bless all nations. To Israel, these foreigners may have been allies or enemies, but to God, they were people who needed to be brought back into relationship with Him and Israel was His primary means of doing so.

Second, these messages reminded the Israelites that God had their back. He had promised Abraham that whoever cursed Israel would pay dearly; these oracles of judgment assured the Israelites of eventual vindication.

Third, these messages to the other nations reminded Israel that Yahweh was not only their king, but the king of all nations. He had the right to judge those nations, just as He had the right to judge Israel. Even more than judgment, God desired to bring those nations into fellowship with Himself (see Isaiah 19:18-25; 66:19-21).

Judgment was the primary theme of the messages preached by the prophets before Judah went into exile in 586 BC. God's people had sinned by failing to love Him and love each other, and they needed to be punished. Sometimes God expressed that judgment as if a plaintiff in court (see Isaiah 3:13-26), or a mourner at a funeral (see Habakkuk 2:6-8), or as if a herald announcing a coming battle (see Hosea 5:8-10). Each time the point was the same, unless Israel repented and returned to God, they would be judged.

The threatened judgment eventually arrived at the hands

of Israel's enemies who overran the northern and southern kingdoms. These conquerors destroyed cities, walls, palaces, even God's temple, and sent the people into exile.

Still worse than the actual destruction was God's estrangement from His people, graphically portrayed in a vision to the prophet, Ezekiel. He witnessed God's throne rising from the temple and departing (see Ezekiel 10-11), abandoning His palace because of the wickedness of His people.

Shorthand for the coming judgment was the phrase, the "Day of Yahweh." This phrase or some variation (such as, "the day of the anger of Yahweh," "Yahweh has a day," "that day," "the day of," "the day when") is used more than 200 times in the prophetic books. It refers to that time when God would personally come to judge the wicked, whether wicked foreign nations or the wicked among God's people. For the righteous, that day was a cause for hope for it meant reward and the renewal of all things.

Although messages of judgment predominate in prophecies delivered prior to the exile, hope was always present. The announcement of judgment itself was not necessarily a statement of what would happen, but what would happen if there was no repentance. The threat of judgment was intended primarily as a call for repentance.

No matter how scathing the judgment, God always offered the hope of a better day, after the punishment. One of my favorite hope-filled passage is found in Amos 9:11-15. These are the final verses of a book that spends most of its time condemning oppression and idolatry:

> [11] "In that day I will restore David's fallen shelter—I will repair its broken walls and restore its ruins—and will rebuild it as it used to be, [12] so that they may possess the remnant of Edom and all the nations that bear my name," declares the

LORD, who will do these things. [13] "The days are coming," declares the LORD, "when the reaper will be overtaken by the plowman and the planter by the one treading grapes. New wine will drip from the mountains and flow from all the hills, [14] and I will bring my people Israel back from exile. They will rebuild the ruined cities and live in them. They will plant vineyards and drink their wine; they will make gardens and eat their fruit. [15] I will plant Israel in their own land, never again to be uprooted from the land I have given them," says the LORD your God.

After all the judgment, God's people will be restored to fellowship with Him. They will live in peace with one another and themselves, becoming the beneficiaries of a harvest so rich the "reaper will be overtaken by the plowman" and the grape juice will flow down from the vineyards like streams.

The prophets also offered the hope of a king from the line of David ("I will restore David's fallen shelter"). This person was referred to as the Anointed One since kings were anointed with oil at their coronation. The Hebrew term for Anointed One is *meshiach*, or Messiah (see Habakkuk 3:13).

Many passages in the prophets identify the Messiah as coming from David's line:

In love a throne will be established; in faithfulness a man will sit on it—one from the house of David—one who in judging seeks justice and speeds the cause of righteousness (Isaiah 16:5).

I will place on his shoulder the key to the house of David; what he opens no one can shut, and what he shuts no one can open (Isaiah 22:22).

"The days are coming," declares the LORD, "when I will raise up for David a righteous Branch, a King who will reign wisely and do what is just and right in the land" (Jeremiah 23:5).

²² I will save my flock, and they will no longer be plundered. I will judge between one sheep and another. ²³ I will place over them one shepherd, my servant David, and he will tend them; he will tend them and be their shepherd. ²⁴ I the LORD will be their God, and my servant David will be prince among them. I the LORD have spoken (Ezekiel 34:22-24).

Afterward the Israelites will return and seek the LORD their God and David their king. They will come trembling to the LORD and to his blessings in the last days (Hosea 3:5).

One prophet even identifies the birthplace of the Messiah as Bethlehem, David's city (see Micah 5:2).

Just as David's reign brought blessings such as security, prosperity, and peace to Israel, the Messiah's reign would be an even greater time of blessing. Isaiah 65:17-25 captures it well:

¹⁷ "See, I will create new heavens and a new earth. The former things will not be remembered, nor will they come to mind. ¹⁸ But be glad and rejoice forever in what I will create, for I will create Jerusalem to be a delight and its people a joy. ¹⁹ I will rejoice over Jerusalem and take delight in my people; the sound of weeping and of crying will be heard in it no more. ²⁰ Never again will there be in it an infant who lives but a few days, or an old man who does not live out his years; the one who dies at a hundred will be thought a mere child; the one who fails to reach a hundred will be considered accursed. ²¹ They will build houses and dwell in them; they will plant vineyards and eat their fruit. ²² No longer will they build houses and others live in them, or plant and others eat. For as the days of a tree, so will be the days of my people; my chosen ones will long enjoy the work of their hands. ²³ They

will not labor in vain, nor will they bear children doomed to misfortune; for they will be a people blessed by the LORD, they and their descendants with them. ²⁴ Before they call I will answer; while they are still speaking I will hear. ²⁵ The wolf and the lamb will feed together, and the lion will eat straw like the ox, and dust will be the serpent's food. They will neither harm nor destroy on all my holy mountain," says the LORD.

Humanity will be in such harmony with God that He will answer before they even call, will hear while they are still speaking (see verse 24). They will be at peace with one another and themselves, unafraid and joyful (see verses 18, 21-22). They will even be at peace with nature (v. 25).

Jeremiah speaks of these days as a new covenant (Jeremiah 31:31-34). This isn't a new covenant in the sense of replacing the one made with Abraham in Genesis 12:1-3; Jeremiah's description of the new covenant makes this clear. The prophet calls it new because it represents the extraordinary fulfillment of the earlier one.

God teaches yet another lesson through the prophets. Not only will the Messiah bring blessings, he will also suffer on behalf of the people. We see this most clearly in Isaiah's description of God's servant. The prophet describes the servant as being rejected, even though he carried Israel's sins.

⁵ But he was pierced for our transgressions, he was crushed for our iniquities; the punishment that brought us peace was on him, and by his wounds we are healed. ⁶ We all, like sheep, have gone astray, each of us has turned to our own way; and the LORD has laid on him the iniquity of us all (Isaiah 53:5-6).

This would be a lesson that many later Israelites would miss.

They expected the Messiah to arrive as a conquering king, not a suffering servant.

The ministry of the prophets delayed God's judgment but could not prevent it. Israel, which began in the rebellion against Solomon's son, Rehoboam, was conquered by the nation of Assyria in 722 BC. Almost a century and a half later, in 586 BC, the Babylonians defeated the southern kingdom, destroyed Jerusalem and the Temple, and sent all but the poorest people into exile.

As we noted in a previous chapter, this exile served to refine God's people. Those who returned, the "righteous remnant" (see Isaiah 10:22), had been chastened and disciplined. They came back much less inclined toward idolatry and much more eager to hear and obey God's law.

Return from Exile

God had promised that the exile would only be temporary. Isaiah had even predicted the name of the person who would be responsible for ending it (see Isaiah 44:28; 45:1, 13). Even still, the sudden turn of events that not only allowed but actually encouraged the "Jews" (the name used for the Israelites beginning around this time) to return home from Babylon left them wide-eyed in amazement.

The Babylonian Empire came to an end in 539 BC at the hands of the Persians. The Persian ruler, Cyrus, had a different strategy for dealing with captured peoples. Unlike the Assyrians and Babylonians who deported conquered peoples, Cyrus returned them to their homelands, helped rebuild their temples, and encouraged them to pray to their gods for Cyrus' success.

And so, beginning in 538 BC, the Jews began to return home. Their initial euphoria gave way to discouragement as they discovered the rigors of rebuilding. Once again, God sent prophets like Haggai, Zechariah and Malachi. This time their message was primarily one of hope, although salted with words of correction.

Buoyed by prophetic encouragement, the Jews rebuilt their society, the city of Jerusalem, and the temple. Although much smaller than the one built by Solomon, Haggai promised that this temple would be even more glorious than the earlier model (see Haggai 2:9). He was right, for centuries later Jesus Himself would visit this second temple.

Haggai's message of hopeful anticipation typified this post-exilic period for the Jews. Their present circumstances were less than ideal. No longer an independent nation with their own king, they were now only a province in the vast Persian Empire. But they knew something better was on the way.

In the Hebrew Bible, the closing books are 1 and 2 Chronicles. These books focus on the lives of David and Solomon. The Chronicler intended this backward look to set the standard for what would come when God intervened on their behalf.

The Jews were right; God would intervene, although it would come in a way they did not expect. Before we explore that intervention, we need to consider what God was doing during the so-called "silent years."

Study Questions

1. What is the difference between the viewing the prophets as foretellers and forth-tellers?

2. Explain what is meant by the assertion, "we always become like what we worship"?

3. How does alienation from God make alienation from others more likely?

4. Why might later Jews have missed the emphasis on the Messiah having to suffer?

Chapter Ten
ANYTHING BUT SILENT
The Intertestamental Period

After the final book of the Old Testament was written, God's plan lay dormant for four centuries. Nothing much happened until John the Baptist appeared in the wilderness, crying out, "Repent, for the Kingdom of God is at hand!" At least, that's how the story is usually told. In fact, although God was not speaking as He had earlier, He continued to work his plan through these four centuries, crucial years for the plan's development.

Jewish history in the time between the testaments

As we noted in the previous chapter, the Jews were permitted to return from exile in Babylon thanks to Cyrus, the king of Persia. They would remain subject to the Persians for the next two centuries. The Jews who returned to Judea, such as Ezra and Nehemiah, were allowed to rebuild Jerusalem and the temple.

Those who returned to Judea, or as the Persian province was now known, Yahud, were not ruled by their own king, but by a Jewish governor who answered to the Persian emperor. For religious matters, they were guided by their high priest. According to the best estimates for this time period, about 30,000 people lived in small, un-walled villages in Yahud. Only about 3,000 lived in and around the city of Jerusalem.

Many other Jews, like Esther and Daniel, did not return but remained in the land of exile where they had already lived for a generation. Still others resettled elsewhere. We know of a Jewish community at Elephantine in Egypt that even built its own temple to Yahweh. In the centuries to come, the Jews would continue to disperse throughout the Mediterranean world, some by choice, some by necessity.

In July of 356 BC a child was born to Philip II, King of Macedon, in the northern part of what is now Greece. This young boy, Alexander, was tutored by Aristotle, the great philosopher. While still a teen, Alexander took up the sword and became one of the greatest military leaders the world has ever seen.

After his father's death, Alexander consolidated his kingdom and began his campaign to defeat the Persians. He accomplished this goal by 333 BC after a series of battles, the most decisive of which took place on the Plains of Issus, not far from the town where the Apostle Paul would one day be born.

Alexander next defeated the Egyptians and moved on to put the final nail in the Persian coffin. He and his army continued east, defeating several kingdoms before finally turning back at the Ganges River in what is now India. He died in Babylon of malaria at age 32.

At the time of his premature death, Alexander the Great had no suitable heir, so his kingdom was divided among his four generals. One of these, Ptolemy, ruled over Egypt and the land of the Jews.

During and immediately after Alexander's reign, many inhabitants of Yahud relocated to other parts of the Macedonian empire. According to Strabo, the first century BC geographer, it was difficult to find a place in the world without a Jewish population. The Jewish philosopher, Philo, writes of no less than a million Jews in Egypt alone. Perhaps as much as 40% of the population of Alexandria, Egypt, was Jewish.

Both those scattered and those who remained discovered the allure of Greek culture. Prior to the Greeks, most rulers subdued conquered peoples by scattering their leaders, those most likely to resist foreign occupation. Alexander's strategy was different. Like a missionary, he exposed the conquered people to the best of Greek culture, including its architecture, government, literature, and philosophy. Thanks to this process, known as Hellenization, the cultures Alexander conquered ended up looking more like his own.

This was also true for the Jews, a reality that led to trouble in the years ahead. Jews adopted the Greek language, Greek architecture and other elements of Hellenism. Those who maintained strict adherence to Judaism, however, had to remain somewhat aloof from this cosmopolitan culture.

For example, the law of Moses prohibited them from participating in activities involving idolatry, such as eating food sacrificed to idols. The Ptolemies (those Greeks who descended from Alexander's general, Ptolemy, and ruled from Egypt) mostly tolerated this Jewish isolationism, granting them a fair degree of autonomy.

This more tolerant period ended when the Jews became subjects of the Seleucid Kingdom beginning around 200 BC. The Seleucid kingdom was also Greek and, like the Ptolemies, had arisen after Alexander's death. The Seleucids ruled from the city of Antioch in Syria.

At first, life under the Seleucids appears to have been manageable for the Jews. It wasn't long, however, before they came under intense pressure to compromise the essential features of what it meant to be Jewish. This pressure led some to rise up in rebellion.

In need of cash, the Seleucids had tried to raid the provincial coffers, including the temple in Jerusalem. Jewish resistance and the political maneuvering that followed led to more and more Jews compromising their religious convictions. It also led to the Seleucid king, Antiochus IV, plundering the temple in Jerusalem and sacrificing a pig on the altar in 169 BC (see 1 Maccabees 1:41-64). Two years later he banned Jewish practices, such as Sabbath observance and circumcision.

All of this was too much for Mattathias, a Jew from the tribe of Levi. He began what we know as the Maccabean revolt against the Seleucids in 167 BC. The name of Mattathias' family was the Hasmoneans, but they were better known as the Maccabees, meaning "hammer," given their reputation as fighters.

Within three years, the Maccabees had liberated Jerusalem and re-consecrated the temple, something Jews still celebrate at Hanukkah (see 1 Maccabees 4:36-61). They eventually regained full political independence, placing the first Jewish king on the throne in Jerusalem in more than 450 years.

This new dynasty, the Hasmonean dynasty, although the fruit of great courage, was a failure from the start. Within decades most Jews were glad to surrender their sovereignty and become subjects of the Roman Empire. That took place in 63 BC when the Roman general, Pompey, entered Jerusalem. Jewish independence may have ended, but their desire for freedom remained.

What in the world was God doing?

What does all this have to do with God's plan? A great deal! All this time, God was actively preparing the world for the coming of Christ, the cornerstone of that plan.

Even more interesting, God was accomplishing this while His people were relatively weak. God was working in and through His people, but He was also working through people who didn't know He existed. God proved His power by using powerful people to do what He wanted.

Take Alexander the Great's sweeping military conquest from Macedon to India. One consequence of this conquest was to establish Greek as the common language for the entire region. Other languages were still spoken, but thanks to Alexander, one could travel nearly 3500 miles, across what is today Greece, Turkey, Egypt, Iraq, Iran, Afghanistan, Pakistan, and India, and always be able to communicate with someone in Greek. Think of the advantages this created when Christians set out as missionaries through these territories to preach the gospel! Imagine how much more difficult that task would be even today.

Another advance in God's plan involved the translation of the Bible. As Greek became the common language, many Jews desired a translation of the Hebrew Bible in Greek. This translation, known as the Septuagint, was produced during the Ptolemaic period. It would later become the preferred Bible of the early Christians. This made it easier for them to use the Bible in missionary work. They could show from the Scriptures in Greek how God's plan was fulfilled in Christ.

The Jews wrote many other books during this time period, some of which were quite influential on the early church. The New Testament author, Jude, even quotes from two of these books (see Jude 9, 14).

Several of the books written during the Intertestamental period, books known as the Apocrypha, were given special status by the early church. Perhaps the best known of these are 1 and 2 Maccabees, which describe the Jewish revolt against the Seleucids. The special status of the Apocrypha led some Christians, such as Roman Catholics, to later consider them as Scripture, while others, such as Protestants, see them only as important witnesses of the Intertestamental period, but not inspired to the same degree as the rest of the Bible.

Another benefit of Hellenization was a common culture. Like a common language, cultural similarities made it easier to explain the gospel. Although each culture retained its unique aspects, Hellenization created enough common ground that the gospel could move essentially unhindered across the length and breadth of the Mediterranean world.

As the Roman Empire grew in power, it absorbed the Greek kingdoms. It has been said that while the Romans conquered the Greeks militarily, the Greeks conquered the Romans culturally. Romans embraced much of Greek culture, such as language, architecture, literature, and philosophy. To this they added their own contributions, including infrastructure. For example, Roman roads were marvels of modern engineering; some of these remain in use today. Travel and communication were greatly facilitated by Roman ingenuity. It is obvious to see how this would have been helpful to the early Christian missionaries.

The Romans also used their military might to maintain what is called the *Pax Romana*, the extended time of peace between the reign of the Emperor Augustus, about two decades before Christ's birth, to the death of the Emperor Marcus Aurelius, in AD 180. This is precisely the time when the Church was beginning and spreading across the Roman world. Here again, God was working out His sovereign plan through powerful people and cultural shifts.

During these so-called "silent" years, the Jews had been spreading out from their land, sometimes voluntarily, sometimes being forced to do so. By the time of Christ, they could be found throughout the Roman world. As the Greek geographer Strabo observed, it was difficult to find a place where the Jews weren't.

This made the spread of the gospel much easier. Now the early Christian missionaries were able to begin their evangelistic work among those who were at least already monotheists. Their Jewish audience already knew about God's plan to use the Jews to bless the Gentiles. The missionaries' main task was to persuade them that Jesus of Nazareth was the cornerstone of that plan.

Alexander's conquests influenced this period in other ways, such as by shifting religious thought in the direction of monotheism. As we pointed out earlier, Jews were essentially alone in the ancient world in their belief in one and only one God. Everyone else believed in a multiplicity of gods, the identity of those gods specific to each region.

The spread of a common culture, thanks to Alexander, led people to consider whether the many gods worshiped by different peoples might actually be the same gods, just worshiped under different names. While not yet monotheism, this view was one step closer to it. Perhaps this transitional step made it possible for Paul's audience in Athens to understand his reference to "an unknown God" (Acts 17:23).

Scholars have noted a shift in culture around this time from very group oriented to more individualistic. They credit Alexander the Great for contributing to this shift. This makes sense, given Alexander's pop star status. (At least one other king tried to capture the "Alexander" factor, picturing himself on his coins with the long flowing hair for which Alexander was known.) If one person can accomplish so much in so little time, the thinking goes, each person must have significance.

Christianity does not deny the importance of the group and never sanctions the hyper-individualism that prevails in Western culture today. It does, however, build on the transition toward individualism in which Alexander played an important part.

Jesus, while remaining part of his group-oriented culture, stepped beyond it and called his disciples to do the same.

> [24]Whoever wants to be my disciple must deny themselves and take up their cross and follow me. [25]For whoever wants to save their life will lose it, but whoever loses their life for me will find it (Matthew 16:24-25).

Thanks to this recognition of the importance of the individual, we understand more clearly that God wants to have a personal relationship with each of us. God used Alexander the Great to help bring about this shift.

What God was doing among His people

God was teaching His people about Himself and His plan throughout the Old Testament and continued these lessons during the time between the testaments. When the Jews returned from exile in Babylon, they better understood the importance of obeying the law of Moses. A group even emerged, the scribes, whose responsibility it was to teach the law to the Jews. Ezra is perhaps the best-known scribe from the post-exilic period.

During the time between the testaments, increasing contact between the Jews and other groups increased the pressure to compromise. The faithful Jews discovered that obedience to the law could be costly, even deadly. Some Jews compromised, choosing to blend in with Greek culture rather than be faithful to their covenant promises. Others remained firm in their faithfulness.

The gymnasium was a significant proving ground for faithfulness. Greeks loved their gymnasiums where they could bathe, exercise, socialize, and talk philosophy. They did this naked, the meaning of the Greek word, *gymnos*. But nakedness revealed whether or not a man had been circumcised, the distinguishing mark of a Jew. This prompted some Jews to undergo a painful operation to reverse their circumcision, allowing them to pass for Gentiles.

Such challenges to remain faithful help explain the situation we meet in the New Testament. There we find the Pharisees, for whom keeping the law had become the primary focus. To insure they kept the law, they expanded it through oral traditions. In their defense, they had seen the dangers of compromise and were determined not to make the same mistake.

Others responded to the clash of cultures by withdrawing and establishing isolated communities. One such group, the Essenes, set up at Qumran near the Dead Sea to live in purity, untainted by compromise. We know them best for the Dead Sea Scrolls, a large collection of documents found in the middle of the last century in nearby caves. The discovery of these scrolls in the mid-1900's was one of the most important archaeological finds ever, allowing us to better understand the Bible.

Although they aren't mentioned by name in the New Testament, the Essenes had a lot of influence on early Christianity. Some speculate that John the Baptist was raised by this community after the death of his elderly parents. His message, and that of John's cousin, Jesus, sound more like the teaching of the Essenes than the Pharisees or other groups.

The Qumran community described the world as either light or dark, righteous or wicked. The two forces were in battle with one another and only by strict purity would the righteous few prevail. We hear little of this sort of talk in the Old Testament, but meet it often in the New. It arises as one way Judaism reacted to

Greek culture during the time between the Testaments.

The Essenes withdrew from culture while John the Baptist and Jesus took this message out among the Jewish people, especially the *am ha'aretz*, the "people of the land." The cousins spoke of the need to repent and of the importance of a piety deeper than what could be found among the Pharisees or Essenes.

God also chose this period to help His people better understand what happens to a person after death. It makes sense that this would become an increasingly important question given the growing emphasis on individual persons and given the fact that some were being martyred for their obedience to the law.

The question of what happens after death was never very important to the Jews. For most of their history they were content to think of death as the natural end of life, followed by Sheol. Neither heaven nor hell, Sheol was just a place you went. While it lacked the joys of life, it also provided a welcomed rest.

The Old Testament contains hints of something more, such as when God tells Daniel,

> ²Multitudes who sleep in the dust of the earth will awake: some to everlasting life, others to shame and everlasting contempt. ³ Those who are wise will shine like the brightness of the heavens, and those who lead many to righteousness, like the stars for ever and ever (Daniel 12:2-3).

Such hints blossomed into certainty in the time between the Testaments. In 2 Maccabees 7, we find the story of seven brothers and their mother, arrested for obedience to the law. The Greek king tries to get them to eat pork, something forbidden in the law. When they refuse, the king has them tortured to death.

As they die, they affirm their faith in a bodily resurrection. One son, with his final breath, addresses the king, "Cruel brute, you may discharge us from this present life, but the King of the world will raise us up, since we die for his laws, to live again for ever" (v. 9 New Jerusalem Bible). Another greeted his torture and death with this confidence, "Heaven gave me these limbs; for the sake of his laws I have no concern for them; from him I hope to receive them again" (v. 11 NJB).

Their mother, who witnessed this horrific scene, encouraged their faithfulness with these words,

> [22] I do not know how you appeared in my womb; it was not I who endowed you with breath and life, I had not the shaping of your every part. [23] And hence, the Creator of the world, who made everyone and ordained the origin of all things, will in his mercy give you back breath and life, since for the sake of his laws you have no concern for yourselves (vv. 22-23 NJB).

This confidence in bodily resurrection, about which the Old Testament is all but silent, is stated as a given in the New. Jesus speaks of going to prepare a place for His followers (see John 14:2-3) and of a day when all will stand before the Throne (see Matthew 25:31-32). Paul expands our understanding of bodily resurrection in passages like 1 Corinthians 15. The Intertestamental period is a crucial phase in the development of this greater understanding of life after death.

God used this period to help His people understand other truths about Himself and His plan, truths that would allow a later generation to comprehend the message of Jesus. During this period, God clarified the nature of sin, evil and suffering. Their experience during this period, especially under the worst Seleucid king, Antiochus IV, revealed that obedience could lead, not to blessing, but to more suffering. The Jews thought long and hard about how to understand their present reality in light of their status as God's covenant people. Such thoughts proved crucial to understanding Jesus' suffering and that of His followers.

One outcome of the Jew's painful experience was to emphasize God's transcendence. This refers to God's otherness from this world, that He is not part of nature, but independent of it. The Jews had always believed God was transcendent. At the dedication of the temple, King Solomon spoke of God as being too big for the heavens to contain, not to mention the temple he had built (see 1 Kings 8:27).

But we can find other passages that speak of God as very up-close and personal, such as when He paid a lunch-time visit to Abraham (see Genesis 18). When that same story was retold by a Jew from the Intertestamental period, it is the angel Michael, not God, who visits Abraham. It was easier for the Jews of this later period to think of God as more distant than close at hand. Imagine the shock when Jesus arrived as Immanuel, "God with us" (see Matthew 1:23)!

During these years, God's people thought a lot about the Messiah. They knew the Old Testament believers, especially the prophets, had anticipated someone in David's line. Their suffering made the need for such a king all the more urgent. Although there were many versions of their hope for the Messiah, the consensus anticipated a king or priestly figure who would bring deliverance from foreign oppression.

The "anything-but-silent" years

As we've seen, God was anything but "silent" during these years. Although He was not, in my opinion, inspiring new biblical books, He continued to communicate with His people in ways that bolstered their courage and clarified their understanding.

Now came the moment God had been waiting for, what the Apostle Paul described as "just the right time" (Romans 5:6). The Divine Teacher had covered the necessary curriculum; the world stage was prepared; God's people were as ready as they would ever be. The King of Kings was at the door of a lowly stable in Bethlehem.

Study Questions

1. Why might God have chosen to work in a more hidden way during these "so-called" silent years?

2. In what other ways was God at work during this time?

3. Why might God have waited until this period to teach His people about the resurrection from the dead?

4. What can you learn from this chapter about how to respond during those seasons when God seems silent?

Chapter Eleven
JESUS: THE KEY TO GOD'S PLAN
PART 1: WHO JESUS WAS

The Gospels

Introduction

When Jesus (incognito) met the disciples shortly after His resurrection, they were confused. They thought they knew how all the pieces of God's plan were supposed to fit together. When Jesus was crucified, nothing made sense.

To lead them out of their confusion, Jesus took them to the Old Testament and "explained to them what was said in all the Scriptures concerning himself" (Luke 24:27). He "opened their minds so they could understand the Scriptures" (Luke 24:45). As they understood the Scriptures, their confusion was transformed into a certainty worth dying for.

Jesus, the key to God's plan

We've probably all had those moments when a great teacher explains something to us in a way that we "get it." Everything becomes clear, like a light being switched on in a dark room. These post-resurrection class sessions demonstrate a master teacher at work, helping the disciples make sense of it all.

But at these moments, Jesus was more than the teacher, He was also the subject. He didn't just explain the Old Testament, He explained how His life—the life He had lived among them for the past three years, including His crucifixion and resurrection—fulfilled the Old Testament (see Luke 24:44).

To say that Jesus fulfilled the Old Testament means that He filled it full of meaning. In their confusion, the Old Testament had become a puzzle, disjointed and lacking any clear picture of God's plan. Jesus explained that He was the picture they were looking for. He was the key, the cover on the box of the jigsaw puzzle. When they saw Him, they saw what God had been pointing toward all along.

We have seen how the Old Testament provides a beautiful account of God's concern for His people, as King, as Teacher, and as the giver of work-arounds. On its own, the Old Testament describes a loving God who longs for a relationship with His people and makes it possible for this to happen.

Jesus filled this beautiful story even more full of meaning by showing how far God was willing to go. In the Old Testament we learned from God the Teacher, but the teachings of Jesus take this divine instruction to a whole new level of understanding.

We learned in the Old Testament that God rules as King, but Jesus reveals that His throne would be a cross. The Old Testament was filled with work-arounds for living in a fallen world. Nearly all of these can be retired by the time Jesus concluded His earthly ministry. Jesus was not just another work-around, He was God's ultimate fix for the problem of alienation. The full solution had arrived in the person of Jesus!

To say that Jesus fulfilled the Old Testament means something more. It means that what those books promised, Jesus delivered. They pointed ahead to something, or rather, to someone, the person of Jesus, the Key to it all.

The Old Testament contained God's promise of salvation—the restoration of the four broken relationships. In His life, death, and resurrection, Jesus kept God's promise. In this chapter and the next we'll look at how Jesus fulfilled the promised salvation by examining who He was, what He said, and what He did.

Who He was[2]

Son of God

God showed up in Jesus. Ever since humanity's relationship with God was broken by sin, God was working to restore that relationship. Work-arounds allowed humans a partial experience of His presence, most especially in the tabernacle and temple.

Then one night, in a Bethlehem stable, God arrived in person as an infant. God came to be with us; that's what the Hebrew word, Immanuel, means, God with us. All the questions about how such a thing could happen shouldn't blind us to the amazing truth that it did happen; God showed up in Jesus.

The story of Jesus can be described in one word, gospel. The four gospels tell the story of the gospel, the good news. Gospel comes from a Greek word, *euangelion*, used to describe an encouraging announcement, such as news of victory in battle or the birthday of the emperor.

That the infinite God took on humanity is the best news ever; how it happened is ultimately a "mystery" (1 Timothy 3:16). Based on the evidence, however, we can say that Jesus was every bit as human as you and I, yet still God. He ate, grew tired, slept, suffered and died, but He also did things only God can do, such as exist from eternity (see John 1:1), forgive sin (see Mark 2:1-12) and rise from the dead.

Early on, Christians understood the mystery of the incarnation (that is, God taking on humanity) as the result of the virgin birth

---

[2] *It would be more accurate to speak of who Jesus is, rather than was. The New Testament makes clear that when Jesus ascended to heaven, He took His resurrected body with Him and retains it to this day. When we speak of who Jesus was, we're emphasizing Jesus' earthly ministry.*

of Christ. That is, Mary became pregnant, but not as a result of sexual intercourse. From the clear teaching of passages like Luke 1:26-38 and Matthew 1:18-25 we know that Jesus had a human mother but not a human father.

This was as shocking and hard to prove in the first century as it is in the twenty-first, but the early Christians didn't back down. About AD 110, Bishop Ignatius of Antioch wrote, "being fully persuaded as touching our Lord that He is truly of the race of David according to the flesh, but Son of God by the Divine will and power, truly born of a virgin."

While we don't know exactly *how* such a thing could happen, we have a pretty good idea *why* it happened. God arrived this way as a sign pointing to Jesus' significance. "Therefore the Lord himself will give you a sign: The virgin will conceive and give birth to a son, and will call him Immanuel" (Isaiah 7:14). God was with us.

The virgin birth also demonstrates the importance of being human. As Saint Augustine wrote, "Men, despise not yourselves: the Son of God became a man; despise not yourselves, women; the Son of God was born of a woman." As we saw at creation, humanity was God's masterpiece, well worth saving.

Because of how Jesus was conceived, He was able to solve the sin problem once and for all. Fully God, He was born without sin (see 2 Corinthians 5:21; Hebrews 4:15). Because fully human, He could live a life of real obedience, remaining sinless, and finally offer Himself as a willing sacrifice for human sin. As God, He could not remain dead for long.

Jesus was the Son of God, but also the Messiah. That is, He was the Anointed One whose coming the Old Testament had predicted. Throughout their history the Israelites had known of great leaders, especially David. When they passed through difficulties, they looked back to David and anticipated someone like David who would deliver them. Many passages in the New Testament, especially Matthew's gospel, acknowledge Jesus as the promised Messiah (for example, see Matthew 1:22-23; 2:15, 23; 4:14-16; 8:17; 12:17-21; 13:35; 21:4-5; 26:56).

Jesus was also recognized as the Wisdom of God. It might sound better to say that Jesus *had* God's wisdom rather than say He *was* God's Wisdom. He certainly had God's wisdom. In fact, no one before or since has lived so completely in the fear of the Lord, with the perfect blend of reverence in relationship that constitutes true wisdom.

While it is true that Jesus had God's wisdom, speaking of Jesus *as* the Wisdom of God allows us to connect Him with what we saw in our earlier chapter on the Book of Proverbs. There Wisdom was present in the beginning and was responsible for creation (see Proverbs 8).

John makes these same assertions when he writes about Jesus, "He was with God in the beginning. Through him all things were made; without him nothing was made that has been made" (John 1:2-3). The Apostle Paul describes Jesus as the wisdom of God (see Colossians 1:15-23) as a way of asserting Christ's divinity and His capacity to reconcile us to God. The Old Testament personified wisdom, but the Gospels reveal that Jesus fulfilled Wisdom. True Wisdom was more than a literary personification; He was a real person who arrived as an infant boy.

In the opening to his gospel, John refers to Jesus as the Word, in Greek, the *Logos* (see John 1:1, 14). This word, *logos*, had a rich background in the ancient world. Some philosophers used it to speak of an impersonal force used by God to create and sustain the world. For John, the *logos* created and sustained the world, but not as an impersonal force. Jesus was God articulating

Himself more clearly to humanity than ever.

In the past, God had spoken to His people—to Abraham, to Moses on Mt. Sinai, through the prophets, but now, through Jesus, God has "spoken to us by his Son, whom he appointed heir of all things, and through whom also he made the universe. The Son is the radiance of God's glory and the exact representation of his being, sustaining all things by his powerful word" (Hebrews 1:2-3a). Because He was God's Word, Jesus was really God.

Son of Man

Jesus was not only God, He was also a human being. His favorite term to describe Himself was "Son of Man." God had earlier used this phrase to refer to the prophet Ezekiel, highlighting the prophet's role as a representative of God's people.

This is probably what Jesus meant to communicate when He chose this way of describing Himself; He understood that His role was to represent humanity. In other words, Jesus didn't just come to earth to undergo a challenging task, a solitary hero on a quest. He came, consciously, to represent the rest of us.

Imagine we are a squadron of soldiers trapped behind enemy lines. We lack the power to free ourselves, but persuade the enemy commander to let one of us fight one of their men. If their man wins, we will surrender. If ours wins, we will all go free. Our chosen soldier will fight, not just for his own sake, but on behalf of us all.

This analogy is not perfect—God didn't need to negotiate with Satan for our release—but it does convey how one person could represent a group. God's plan for full-reconciliation involved entrusting one Man with the task of undoing the effects of sin, like the untangling of a knot. Jesus was that man, the Son of Man, Mr. Human.

I had to use an analogy to describe this concept of how one person could act on behalf of a group because our culture is heavily oriented toward the individual. We're taught that each of us should act on his or her own behalf. I must make my own decisions and depend on myself alone. There are still a few places, like the military, where we recognize that one person's actions affect the whole group. But for the most part, it's "every man for himself."

In the ancient world, people were much more accustomed to think of themselves as part of a group, rather than just as individuals. So, for example, when the jailer in Philippi decided to become a Christian as a result of Paul's testimony, his whole household did as well (see Acts 16:27-34).

This is what the Apostle Paul meant by referring to Jesus as the second Adam (see Romans 5:14-19; 1 Corinthians 15:21-22, 45). The first Adam had led humanity into the disaster that follows disobedience and his disobedience brought disaster on us all. The obedience of the last Adam would undo that disaster and lead us into blessing.

Sin entered the world by disobedience; it would be rendered powerless by a perfect example of obedience. As Paul wrote to the Romans, "For just as through the disobedience of the one man the many were made sinners, so also through the obedience of the one man the many will be made righteous" (Romans 5:19).

Jesus made it very clear that His ministry was not His idea; He was only doing what God asked Him to do. "I have come down from heaven," He explained, "not to do my will but to do the will of him who sent me" (John 6:38).

When His disciples offered Him food they had brought, Jesus replied, "My food is to do the will of him who sent me and to finish his work" (John 4:34). Jesus had an appetite for obedience.

Toward the end of His life, Jesus warned the disciples that the "prince of this world," Satan, would soon subject Jesus to the extreme test of suffering and death. Jesus knew things were about to become awful, but He was committed to obey God to the very end. As He explained, "so that the world may learn that I love the Father and do exactly what my Father has commanded me" (John 14:30-31). He knew what was coming but continued to obey. God was using Jesus' amazing example of obedience to unravel the knot of sin which had been tied tightly by disobedience.

Sin entered the world by a lack of faith; Mr. Human lived a life of perfect faith. If only Adam and Eve had trusted God, they would have experienced everything they desired and avoided the catastrophic consequences of disobedience. They failed for lack of faith.

We have seen throughout the Old Testament the high priority God places on faith. Hebrews 11 is known as the Hall of the Heroes of Faith because it tells of many Old Testament believers who accomplished great things by trusting in God.

The greatest hero of faith is Jesus. He trusted God throughout His life. When tempted by Satan at the beginning of His ministry, Jesus refused to turn stones into bread; instead He trusted God to provide. When rejected by the religious leaders, those who were supposed to represent God, Jesus maintained His faith in His Heavenly Father.

His greatest act of faith was to allow Himself to be killed. Where there is life, there's hope, a chance to escape. But death marks the point of no return; after that He would be completely powerless. Yet He willingly allowed Himself to be arrested, convicted, and sentenced to death.

The final temptation to doubt came as Jesus hung on the cross. In His last moments, He felt Himself abandoned by God, the very God He had followed in faithful obedience. In His grief He cried out, "My God, my God, why have you forsaken me?" (Mark 15:34).

These were not Jesus' final words. With His last breath Jesus uttered what may be His most powerful affirmation of faith, "Father, into your hands I commit my spirit" (Luke 23:46). He still believed God was His Father who would do what was best. Jesus had done all He could to faithfully carry out His part in God's plan; if that plan were to succeed, it was now entirely up to God.

The Bible talks often about those who *live* by faith (see Habakkuk 2:4; Romans 1:17; 2 Corinthians 5:7; Galatians 3:11; Hebrews 10:38); Jesus showed how to *live and die* by faith. Doubting God's Word brought terrible suffering into this world. God used Jesus' faith, including His faith in the midst of terrible suffering, to bring about the salvation that would eventually end all suffering.

We have seen that Jesus' obedience and faith helped untie the knot created by Adam and Eve's disobedience and doubt. Let's explore how the actions of the Son of Man, our Representative, reversed the curse.

Reconciliation with God

This curse produced disharmony in the four key relationships; it would be reversed by One who lived a life of perfect harmony in those relationships. No other human being ever lived in such complete fellowship with God, with others, with self, and with the natural world.

Jesus lived a sinless life. He was born in such a way that He did not inherit a sinful nature. Yet He was still capable of sinning, otherwise there would have been no point in His being tempted (see Mark 1:12; 14:32-42). If He had no choice but to obey, then His obedience doesn't count for much.

Jesus was sinless because He chose to keep the law. His enemies tried to find something in His life that they could use against Him, some broken command, but they couldn't. He made them furious by breaking some of their man-made rules, but broke none of God's commandments. During His final trial, the only way they could win a conviction was to use lying witnesses.

He not only kept all the commandments, Jesus lived consistently according to the spirit of the law, the spirit of love. Somebody asked Jesus to name the most important commandment in the law. He answered that there were two: love for God and love for one's neighbor. These two are inseparable and the whole law depends on them (see Matthew 22:36-40).

Jesus did what no one else has been able to do before or since: He loved God with His whole heart, soul, mind, and strength, and loved His neighbor as Himself. There never was a moment when Jesus allowed any other loyalty to eclipse His love for God. Even His love for His mother, the one person on earth who knew Him best, could not compare to the love Jesus had for His Heavenly Father.

Reconciliation with others

Jesus not only lived in harmony with God, He also lived in harmony with others. Obviously, this doesn't mean an absence of conflict. We see this harmony, not in how others treated Him, but how He treated others.

No one ever loved others the way Jesus did. People were drawn to Him, especially those who lived on the margins of society: women, children, the poor, sick, and needy. And when they came, He made time for them. He touched them. He saw their need and met it, whether that was food for the hungry, healing for the diseased and alienated, or significance for the insignificant.

Even when He was rejected and abandoned, He forgave. He explained to His disciples that the greatest act of love is to voluntarily surrender one's life for another (see John 15:13), which is exactly what He did. One of His final cries from the cross was to ask God to forgive those who had put Him to death (see Luke 23:34).

Reconciliation with self

No human ever experienced such peace within Himself as Jesus. We can see this inner peace in His calm demeanor, even in the midst of storms (for example, see Mark 4:35-41; 6:45-52). His inner peace was evident when accused. Jesus refused to give in to the temptation to preserve Himself at any cost (see Matthew 27:14).

Perhaps we see His inner peace most clearly during the last week of Jesus' life. He experienced the shame of betrayal, abandonment, and denial by his followers. Although welcomed into town on Sunday, by Friday those in Jerusalem were crying for His death, with the religious leaders eager to bring this about. He was arrested, tried, and condemned to death on a cross, a form of execution reserved for the worst of the worst.

Then they hung Him on the cross, naked. Most artists add a loin cloth, but victims of crucifixion hung naked, completely exposed. Adam and Eve realized their nakedness and tried to cover themselves. Jesus felt this shame and humiliation like any human would, but was at such peace with Himself that He did not allow shame to deter Him from His mission.

Reconciliation with nature

Jesus also experienced a relationship with the natural world unlike anyone before or since. As we saw in chapter 1, God created humans to be at home in creation, masters of its secrets and able to employ those secrets on behalf of others. With the arrival of sin, the world became a harder place to experience this sense of calling.

If anyone ever knew a calling on His life, it was Jesus. He knew God had sent Him into the world to fulfill the promises made in the Old Testament and accomplish God's plan. Nothing could distract Him from His mission.

Others before Him had worked miracles, but we know of no miraculous power like that of Jesus. Each of His miracles provides an example of how a fallen world, a world insensitive to humans, can become an ally.

Jesus should have sunk when He stepped onto the surface of the Sea of Galilee. Instead, He was able to turn the water into a walkway, allowing Him to walk where He wanted.

Because a little bit of bread and fish can't feed many people, those who had gathered to hear Jesus should have experienced hunger. Instead, Jesus' miraculous power multiplied that little bit of food to feed everyone present, with plenty left over. Jesus' ability to work miracles demonstrates a mastery of nature's secrets and a passion to use those secrets to help others.

Jesus lived as no other human ever lived, completely reconciled to God, others, self, and the world. Through this life of perfect love, God was able to restore the broken relationships experienced by all. We saw earlier that all of humanity had been tied up by the sin of one man, Adam. Through Jesus, the Son of God, Messiah, Wisdom of God, Logos, and Son of Man, the knot of sin was unraveled. As Jesus promised, "if the Son sets you free, you will be free indeed" (John 8:36).

We have explored this crucial moment in God's plan from one perspective, by considering Jesus' nature. Yet there is much more to see. We return to the Gospels, this time to reflect on Jesus' remarkable words and actions.

Study Questions

1. How would you explain to a new Christian how Jesus fulfilled the Old Testament?

2. Spend time reflecting on Christ's own testimony to His divinity (i.e. Matthew 28:18; Luke 22:69-70; John 8:58; 10:30, 38; 12:45; 14:7-10; 16:15; 17:5, 24). How do these passages help you better understand Jesus as the Son of God?

3. I compared Jesus' role as our representative to a soldier fighting on behalf of his comrades. In what other ways might one illustrate how Jesus represented us?

4. In what other ways do you see in the Gospels how Jesus was perfectly reconciled to God, others, self, and nature?

Chapter Twelve

JESUS, THE KEY TO GOD'S PLAN
PART 2: WHAT JESUS SAID AND DID
The Gospels

Introduction

Trying to describe Jesus is a challenge. I can understand why we have four gospels rather than just one; no single picture can do Him justice. John must have felt this way when he came to the end of writing his gospel. He concludes with these words, "Jesus did many other things as well. If every one of them were written down, I suppose that even the whole world would not have room for the books that would be written" (John 21:25).

In the previous chapter we began to consider Jesus as the key to God's reconciling plan. We looked at who He was, both Son of God and Son of Man. We have come to know who He was largely by what He said and did; in this chapter we'll reflect on Christ's words and actions.

What He said

The word on the street was that no teacher ever taught like Jesus (see John 7:46). His listeners hung on every word, and when He finished, they were amazed. They marveled at his teaching "because he taught as one who had authority, and not as their teachers of the law" (Matthew 7:29).

The teachers of the law were dependent on the teachings of other teachers, while Jesus depended on the authority of His Bible (our Old Testament) and the character of His Heavenly

Father. But the "authority" they heard in His words rested on something more: what He said was true.

Truth has a way of making itself known. It's not foolproof—sometimes we can be convinced that something is true when it isn't—but truth generally has a way of authenticating itself, especially the truth about ourselves and God. Our souls are like a tuning fork. When touched by truth they ring with a recognizable tone.

When we hear that we are made in God's image but have fallen beneath that image because of sin, it rings true. This truth explains why humans are capable of such remarkable accomplishments but tilt toward turning those accomplishments to self-advantage against others.

To hear that God is present everywhere rings true. It explains our conscience and our instinct to cry out to Him when we're in trouble. When we're told that God is good, it makes sense at a deep level, so much sense that we keep trusting in the goodness of God even when we're suffering. Capital "T" Truth "connects the dots," providing just the right perspective, the one that brings clarity and conviction.

Jesus' teaching rang true in the ears of His hearers, but also in their eyes. What they heard Jesus say about God's love and holiness, they saw embodied before them in Jesus, God's Son. This is why Jesus is able to refer to Himself as "the way, and the truth, and the life" (John 14:6).

Of course, not all Jesus' audience approved of what they heard and saw. The religious leaders felt threatened, responding with jealousy. Even the crowds who had listened with amazement to Jesus' truth later shouted for His death.

This didn't surprise Jesus. He knew you could only discern the truth if you had "ears to hear" (Mark 4:9, 23). The ability of your soul to ring in response to truth depends on your ongoing desire to hear it more than anything else. Otherwise, the grip of self-interest will sooner or later deaden any sound.

Jesus taught the people in such a way that made them think of Moses. He did this intentionally, not to borrow from Moses' authority, but to show that His own authority was superior, even to that of the greatest teacher of Israel (see Hebrews 3).

Jesus' greatest sermon is called the Sermon on the Mount and is found in Matthew 5 and 6 (and in a slightly different version in Luke 6:17-49). The location is intentional; as Moses went up on a mountain (Mt. Sinai) to receive the law, Jesus went up on a mountain to deliver a new law.

Jesus spends a fair bit of the Sermon on the Mount talking about the law of Moses. He assures His hearers that He isn't opposed to this law. Those who keep it will be blessed and those who break it will be punished (see Matthew 5:17-20). Later He will affirm the eternal truthfulness of the law's essence: love for God and neighbor (see Matthew 22:37-40).

But after affirming the law of Moses, Jesus proceeds with authority to clarify the law (see Matthew 5:21-22) and even establish a new commandment regarding divorce that sets aside the old one (see Matthew 5:31-32). Is He contradicting Himself?

No, for while affirming the essence of the law of Moses, Jesus also emphasizes its purpose. The 613 commands given by Moses were not meant to be permanent, but only a work-around. They all pointed to Him, the Son of Man, who would fulfill the law in a way no one else could or would. Note Jesus' words in Matthew 5:17: "Do not think that I have come to abolish the Law or the Prophets; I have not come to abolish them but to fulfill them."

Jesus' style of teaching was very different from that of Moses. The latter conveyed mostly legal judgments while Jesus mostly told stories. To be more precise, Jesus generally spoke in parables and some of these took the form of stories.

The essence of a parable is to explain something less well known by comparing it to something better known. Jesus' audience knew about things like sheep and fishing and lost coins, so He used such things to explain the Kingdom of God, something about which they needed to know more.

Learning that Jesus was a great teacher who stooped to the level of His listeners should sound familiar. Like Father, like Son. Throughout the Old Testament God sounded like a kindergarten teacher, helping His people understand their lessons.

Jesus' teaching in parables displays the same concern to put the truth at a level where anyone could find it. Even more, Jesus' life was a parable in action. God made Himself known by arriving in human form.

If Jesus' favorite form of teaching was the parable, the favorite topic of His parables was the Kingdom of God (or as it's sometimes known, the Kingdom of Heaven). The Kingdom of God is the realm where God rules. Although He is king over everything, not everyone acknowledges Him as king. Jesus came to announce that this was about to change, for "the Kingdom of God has come near" (Mark 1:15).

The Kingdom of God exists wherever the four broken relationships are being restored. When a person acknowledges God as their rightful king, turns from their rebellion, accepts the King's forgiveness, and loyally obeys, the Kingdom of God has come. Reconciliation has taken place between that person and God.

When a person is enabled to love their enemy, to forgive those who have wronged them, to show mercy to all, and when that person becomes a peacemaker, the Kingdom of God has come. This person is experiencing human to human reconciliation.

When I can live in humility and meekness, without shame or guilt, patient in suffering, even rejoicing in persecution, I am experiencing the Kingdom of God as I experience reconciliation with myself.

Jesus promises that those who are part of His Kingdom "inherit the earth" (Matthew 5:5). Like Jesus, they hunger and thirst for righteousness even more than for food (see Matthew 5:6). They live with the noblest calling, to be the salt of the earth, savoring society, and as the light of the world, enlightening those in darkness (see Matthew 5:13-14). For people like this, the Kingdom of God has come, for they have been reconciled to creation.

Like His Heavenly Father, Jesus became a teacher, and like His Father, He stooped to make the truth accessible to everyone. Jesus' words reflected the Father's desire that every human being experience total healing.

What He did

Jesus lived about as many years as Alexander the Great. Alexander was raised in a palace and enjoyed all the benefits of palatial living. Jesus was raised by a peasant couple in a backwater town in a backwater province of the Roman empire. Alexander was taught by one of the greatest minds who ever lived, the philosopher Aristotle. We know nothing of Jesus' formal training, if He had any.

By the time Alexander was 20, he was ruling as king. At that age, Jesus was probably working as a carpenter; we're not sure. By age 25, Alexander had won decisive victories over the Persian and Egyptian kingdoms. When Jesus was 25 He was probably still working as a carpenter, we're not sure.

By age 30, Alexander had founded multiple cities and named them after himself. At about the same age, Jesus left Nazareth to begin an itinerant ministry of teaching and healing.

Alexander died at age 33, one of the greatest generals and most powerful individuals who had ever lived. Jesus died at about that same age, having been betrayed by one of his followers, abandoned by the others, rejected by the religious leaders, and crucified by the Roman government.

Yet Jesus accomplished infinitely more in his life than even Alexander the Great. In that span of 33 years, only three of which were spent in active ministry, Jesus accomplished what God had been preparing for since the Garden of Eden.

In the previous chapter we described how Jesus, as our Representative, obeyed and trusted in God. His faith and obedience counteracted the doubt and disobedience that had marred humanity from its early days. Everything Jesus did was in obedience to and with faith in His Heavenly Father.

We also talked about Jesus' miracles as a demonstration of His reconciliation with the natural world. By healing the sick, casting out demons, multiplying food, turning water into wine, walking on water, calming storms, raising the dead, and much more, Jesus was anticipating what life will be like when this world is no longer subject to the curse.

But these miracles were also ways Jesus showed love for God's children. Throughout the Old Testament, God responded to the needs of His people by working miracles, the deliverance from Egyptian bondage being the most remarkable. Many times in the gospels we read of Jesus being moved with compassion to work a miracle. Like Father, like Son.

Jesus was also a man of prayer. We find Him going off to pray in the morning (see Mark 1:35) and in the evening (see Mark 6:46-47). At least on one occasion, likely on many, Jesus spent an entire night in prayer (see Luke 6:12). He not only prayed in private, but also in public (see Matthew 11:25; Luke 3:21; John 11:41; 17:1). Prayer seems to have been His way of dealing with the pressures of ministry (see Luke 5:15-16; 9:18; 22:41-42).

As we learn from Jesus how to pray (see Luke 11:1-13; Matthew 6:6), as we listen to Him pray, and watch Him going off to pray in private, we recognize how important prayer is for living a life in harmony with God. We realize that being in harmony with ourselves and others flows from a life of prayer. We understand that our sense of calling is solidified as a result of communion with God.

But we also learn something else, something about God. Until Jesus, the Jews viewed God as a powerful king. During the time between the testaments, this powerful king grew distant. Jesus introduced them to the reality that God was even more like a father. He modeled for them, and for us, that the sovereign God was also our Daddy, or in the language used by Jesus, *Abba* (see Mark 14:36; Romans 8:15; Galatians 4:6).

All the gospel writers understood that the most important years of Jesus' life were the three years of ministry, and the last week of His life was the key to that ministry. They focused their attention on the events between His triumphal entry into Jerusalem on one Sunday, and His resurrection on the next Sunday.

Jesus suffered terribly in the last four days of that last week. Even before they hung Him on the cross, Jesus experienced tremendous physical suffering, including multiple beatings.

He also experienced the emotional suffering of being betrayed and abandoned by those close to Him, rejected by the religious leaders, and mocked as a fraud when He knew Himself to be the Truth. We cannot begin to understand the agony of what He experienced in the Garden of Gethsemane (see Mark 14:32-42).

Jesus suffered to transform our suffering. This was part of God's plan to turn suffering from being an effect of sin into a cause of something better. No one wants to suffer, but if suffering can lead to a better life, we are willing to endure it. Think childbirth.

Jesus showed that suffering can lead to something better, eternally better. Our sufferings can enable us to strengthen others in their suffering (see 2 Corinthians 1:3-5), and can help us become more like Jesus (see Romans 8:17; Philippians 3:10; 1 Peter 4:13). Because Jesus suffered, our suffering will never be without meaning.

Jesus was born to die and He knew it (see Matthew 20:28). He lived His whole life so that when that moment came, He could surrender His final breath without regret. He even knew how He would die, by the most torturous form of execution then imaginable, crucifixion (see John 12:32-33).

Jesus knew that God would use His death to accomplish salvation, the reconciliation of humans to God, to each other, to themselves, and to creation. He compared Himself to a good shepherd who lays down his life for his sheep (see John 10:11, 15, 17). He was a kernel of wheat, He said, that needed to fall to the ground and die so it could produce many more seeds (see John 12:24). On the night before He was arrested, Jesus spoke of His blood being shed to establish the new covenant about which the prophet had spoken (see Luke 22:20; Jeremiah 31:31).

How did the death of Jesus accomplish salvation and thereby fulfill God's plan? Over the centuries following Christ's death,

Christians offered different explanations for how the cross accomplishes its goal. Having a variety of explanations makes sense, given the limitless blessings unfolding from this tragedy.

Likely the earliest understanding saw the cross setting us free from slavery to sin, liberating us. Jesus used the language of ransom (see Mark 10:45), something one pays to a kidnapper to release a hostage. The Apostle Paul also used this language when he described Christians as being "bought at a price" (1 Corinthians 6:20; see Ephesians 1:7). The cross accomplished our liberation.

A later explanation focused on how sin had upset the moral balance of the universe God created. We saw this in the Garden of Eden as the whole of God's perfect paradise, not just humans, was disrupted by human sin. We see this today in the way sin destroys lives, relationships, even whole societies. This is what the Apostle John meant when he wrote, "sin is lawlessness" (1 John 3:4). As the sin of the first Adam led to moral chaos, the obedience to death of the Second Adam led to the restoration of moral order.

Others have pointed out that sin represents an offense against God. A holy God can't just overlook sin; He must punish it or else He becomes complicit with the sinner. In the Old Testament, God established the sacrificial system to provide a work-around for this problem. The sacrifices themselves didn't automatically wipe out the sin, but were vicarious, offered in place of the sinner. God's grace accepted the repentance and faith of the person offering the sacrifice and forgave the sin. The cross provided vicarious atonement for our sin.

The biggest problem with the sacrificial system was that it could never cover the full cost of sin. There weren't enough animals to erase the stain. To do this would require a very special offering.

Enter Jesus, "the Lamb of God who takes away the sin of the world" (John 1:29). He was not only divine but also a sinless human, which meant His voluntary death was the perfect sacrifice to erase the stain, repay the debt, and restore humanity's relationship once and for all (see Colossians 2:13-14). As the writer of Hebrews described it, "we have been made holy through the sacrifice of the body of Jesus Christ once for all" (Hebrews 10:10).

We are given at least one other explanation to explain how the cross accomplishes God's plan. The cross provides a God-sized example of God's love. "God so loved the world that he gave his one and only son" (John 3:16). Christ died so that everyone would see God's love and be drawn to Him. "And I," Jesus said, "when I am lifted up from the earth, will draw all people to myself" (John 12:32). The cross is an example of how much God loves us.

Liberation, **O**rder, **V**icarious atonement, **E**xample, however you explain it, the cross spells LOVE. In whatever ways the cross accomplished God's plan, God's love was the reason for it. It was God's idea, not ours. It was accomplished at His expense; He paid it all. All we can do is accept it and live in light of its effects.

As much as the cross accomplished, it would have fallen short of God's goal if Jesus had remained dead. He had to rise to destroy death and defeat the enemy of our souls. When we looked at the Israelites' deliverance from Egypt, we saw that God accomplished this first by releasing them from their slavery through the tenth plague, the Angel of Death. But there was further deliverance when God destroyed the Egyptian army in the Red Sea.

Something like this happened at Jesus' tomb. He has already provided the perfect Passover Lamb as the ransom to release us; by rising from the dead He defeated the one who holds the power of death. Speaking of Jesus, the writer of Hebrews says, "Since the children have flesh and blood, he too shared in their humanity so that by his death he might break the power of him who holds the power of death—that is, the devil—and free those who all their lives were held in slavery by their fear of death" (Hebrews 2:14-15).

The really remarkable thing about the resurrection wasn't that someone rose from the dead. That had happened before. Jesus' resurrection was truly remarkable because it was God's public declaration that Jesus was who He claimed to be, the Son of God and promised Messiah. The resurrection meant the central moment in God's plan had finally come, salvation had arrived. Death had been defeated and with it, our mortal enemy as well.

Death had been the punishment for sin, but with the resurrection, death is dead. Even though people continue to die, Jesus' resurrection means that death no longer has the last word. As Jesus told Martha, "I am the resurrection and the life. The one who believes in me will live, even though they die; and whoever lives by believing in me will never die" (John 11:25-26).

It was when the disciples witnessed the risen Christ that things began to make sense for them. They understood more clearly what Jesus had said and done once they saw Him alive again. They realized Christ's resurrection marked God's stamp of approval, not only on Jesus, but also on the plan which Jesus fulfilled; Jesus was the key to explain the puzzle.

The curse of sin that had kept us alienated from God, from each other, from self, and from our true calling in this world was broken; over time it would grow progressively weaker. That Peter understood this is clear from these words: "Praise be to the God and Father of our Lord Jesus Christ! In his great mercy he has given us new birth into a living hope through the resurrection of Jesus Christ from the dead" (1 Peter 1:3).

Before we close this chapter, we need to examine the very last thing Jesus did before leaving this earth. He ascended into heaven. We might not think of this as very important, but we would be mistaken. Jesus departed upward into the clouds to provide further confirmation to His disciples that He was who He claimed to be.

Jesus' ascension connects His ministry with the work of the Holy Spirit who would soon descend to complete God's redemptive plan. (We'll say more about this in the next chapter). It wasn't just that Jesus went up (see Acts 1:2, 11) and the Spirit came down (see Acts 2:2), it was that the Spirit came down *because* Jesus went up. This is how Peter explained it to the crowd on the day the Spirit arrived: "Exalted to the right hand of God, he [Jesus] has received from the Father the promised Holy Spirit and has poured out what you now see and hear" (Acts 2:33).

By ascending, Jesus assured His followers He would be praying for them. He didn't just go into heaven, He ascended, as Peter pointed out, to the "right hand of God." This phrase expresses Jesus' privileged position in heaven, with access to God's "ear," so to speak. In Jesus' ascension we gain the assurance that the One who loved us enough to die for us is now where He can provide help whenever we need it.

Finally, Jesus' ascension assures us that He intends to return. As the disciples stood gazing up into the cloud that had hidden their master, an angel appeared and asked, "why do you stand here looking into the sky? This same Jesus, who has been taken from you into heaven, will come back in the same way you have seen him go into heaven" (Acts 1:11).

During His first visit to earth, Jesus accomplished everything

God asked Him to do. But God's plan would unfold over time. Like D-Day in World War II, the enemy had been dealt a fatal blow, but it would take time until the war was over. Jesus' second coming marks the last stage of God's plan when full reconciliation will be accomplished.

The unfolding of God's plan was put into the hands of God's Spirit. Up to this point the Spirit has remained somewhat hidden. The next leg of our flight reveals the Spirit's dramatic arrival, the power He releases in the lives of ordinary people, and the amazing difference the Spirit's power can make.

Study Questions

1. Which is your favorite of Jesus' parables? Why?

2. What do you think of this claim: "The Kingdom of God exists wherever the four broken relationships are being restored"?

3. How would you explain to a new Christian how the cross reconciles us to God?

4. Spend time reflecting on the life and words of Jesus. Write out a prayer, expressing your gratitude to God for what He did in Christ.

Chapter Thirteen
GOD'S PLAN UNFOLDING
The Book of Acts

Introduction

To say that Jesus is the key to God's plan of salvation means that everything written in the Old Testament points to Him. He is the One who would bring the long-awaited and much needed reconciliation. Everything written before Him points toward Him; everything written after points back to Him.

After His resurrection, when the disciples finally understood who He was, they assumed God's plan would move quickly to its completion. Jesus informed them that the end would happen, but not right away. God's plan would unfold over time and they would have an important part to play in that unfolding.

The rest of the New Testament reveals what Jesus had in mind. The Book of Acts tells the story of how the gospel—the good news about Jesus—spread across the Roman Empire.

After Acts we find a collection of letters, many of them written by the Apostle Paul, to gatherings of Christians scattered throughout the Empire. These letters help us understand something more of God's plan of salvation and how it worked itself out in the lives of these Christians.

The last book in the New Testament, Revelation, points forward to the time when Jesus will return. Its purpose, however, is not primarily to predict the future, but to help the early Christians know how to live in their present in light of what the future holds.

The acts of the Holy Spirit

The gospels end with Jesus bidding farewell to His followers. Those followers numbered a little more than a hundred, all clustered in and around the city of Jerusalem. Over the next thirty years or so, Christ-followers would be found as far as Syria, Cyprus, Egypt, all of Asia Minor (now Turkey), Greece, most of Italy and what is now Spain. The number of adherents would expand from around a hundred to hundreds of thousands. The remarkable story of how the gospel exploded with such power is told in the Book of Acts.

This book is often referred to as The Acts of the Apostles. This makes sense because it describes the ministries of the three main apostles, James, Peter and Paul. But the real hero in this book isn't human. It is the Spirit of God.

The Holy Spirit (also known as the Spirit of Jesus) is the third member of the Trinity. He[3] is not an impersonal force—an "it"—but a "person." His job is to put into effect the plan God designed and prepared for, the plan in which Jesus plays the central role. Everything that follows in the New Testament up to the present involves the Spirit executing what God prepared for and Jesus made possible.

Before ascending to heaven, Jesus instructed His followers to wait in Jerusalem until they had received the Spirit. Only then should they begin their work of telling others about Him (see Acts 1:4-5). Jesus knew that without the Spirit's help, their mission would fail, but by the power of the Spirit, they would succeed (see Acts 1:8).

Very wisely, they obeyed Jesus' command and remained waiting in Jerusalem. A short while later, while gathered praying in an

---

[3] *We use the masculine gender, he, only for convenience. The Holy Spirit, like God the Father, has no gender.*

upstairs room on the Jewish festival of Pentecost, the Spirit came down in dramatic fashion (see Acts 2). They heard the sound of a strong wind and saw a flame that divided and rested on each of them. Remarkably, each was given the ability to speak in a language he or she had never learned.

God's choice to mark the Spirit's arrival with the sound of wind makes sense. The word for Spirit in Greek, *pneuma*, can also be translated wind or breath. But why use the symbolism of fire and unknown languages, and why arrive on Pentecost?

Pentecost was one of three pilgrimage festivals observed by the Jews. This explains the extraordinarily large crowd present in Jerusalem at that time. Pentecost was a day to celebrate the first produce of the harvest. As a result of the Spirit's coming on that day, more than 3000 people became followers of Jesus. How fitting that it should happen on Pentecost, the day of "first fruits." These new believers would return home to proclaim the gospel across the Roman Empire.

During the years between the Old and New Testament, Pentecost came to also be associated with the giving of the law to Moses. Since those gathered in this upstairs room on Pentecost were Jewish, the law of Moses was likely on their minds.

To make sure the law was on their minds, God added the fire and languages. By this time these two phenomena had come to be associated with the giving of the law. Philo, the Jewish philosopher born in 25 BC, described the scene on Mt. Sinai:

> Then from the midst of the fire that streamed from heaven there sounded forth to their utter amazement a voice, for the flame became articulate speech in the language familiar to the audience, and so clearly and distinctly were the words formed by it that they seemed to see rather than hear them.

The law had been God's greatest revelation until Jesus. In that law, God had revealed His will, but in Jesus, God revealed Himself. And now, in fulfillment of Jesus' promise (see John 16:7-15), God's Spirit was arriving to dwell in every believer. Jesus could only be present in one place at a time and only temporarily, but now God's Spirit would be present in every believer, everywhere, forever.

Jesus promised that the Spirit would remind the disciples what Jesus had taught them. When God revealed the law, it had to be taught to the people by the priests, but when God revealed Himself in the Spirit, it became possible for each of us to know Him and His will for us.

This helps explain the ability to speak in another language. One might think that this ability was given to enable the gospel to spread among the people who spoke that language. In fact, that probably wasn't necessary. Since everyone already spoke Greek, that was the only language needed.

The disciples' ability to speak in other languages was meant to reveal, as the onlookers said, "the wonders of God in our own tongues" (Acts 2:11). God wanted them to know His great power, but something more. He wanted them to be aware that He knew their "own" language, their "mother tongue," their "heart language."

Language isn't just a currency in which we do business, it's a path to the deepest part of us. God wanted them to know how well He knew them, that He understands their particular culture, and that the message of Christ would fit into that culture and make it infinitely richer.

The spread of the gospel

Empowered by the Spirit, the gospel took off. Jesus had

promised it would go from Jerusalem, to all Judea and Samaria, and then "to the ends of the earth" (Acts 1:8). That describes well the path by which the gospel spread.

The first seven chapters of Acts take place in Jerusalem where the church grew exponentially, though not without paying a price. Acts 8 describes the persecution growing more serious, thanks to the maniacal zeal of Saul of Tarsus. Many of the Christians scattered into the surrounding areas, taking the gospel with them. Instead of extinguishing the fire of the gospel, the church's enemies actually spread it.

At this point the gospel crossed another barrier, not geographical, but cultural. The church up to this point was entirely Jewish, but God sent the Apostle Peter to the home of a Gentile (a non-Jew) who accepted Peter's message and was baptized into the Christian faith.

The conversion of this Gentile, Cornelius, occasioned some controversy for it required Peter to violate Jewish customs by eating with Gentiles. Cornelius was a "God-fearer," that is, a Gentile who had taken steps to align his lifestyle with Jewish practices. After Peter explained how God had orchestrated this visit, his critics were satisfied, at least for the moment.

Cornelius' conversion was just the first of many among Gentiles, arousing no little controversy within the church. But this move from a mission by Jews among Jews to one that saw the gospel being communicated by Jewish believers to Gentiles was just what God had in mind when He called Abraham (see Genesis 12:1-3). There He promised that through Abraham's offspring, all nations would be blessed. The greatest blessing had arrived in the gospel's good news.

Perhaps emboldened by news of the gospel spreading to a Gentile, some Christians began to preach with great success to the Gentiles in the city of Antioch. "The Lord's hand was with them, and a great number of people believed and turned to the Lord" (Acts 11:21). Although this raised the controversy to a new level of urgency, the gospel continued to spread throughout Asia Minor, then to Greece and Rome and beyond.

The growth and expansion of the church across the Roman world was clearly a work of the Holy Spirit. Miracles abounded, including healings, visions, deliverance from prison, and several instances of people being raised from the dead; people even died for lying to the Holy Spirit (see Acts 5:1-14).

One of the greatest miracles was the courage God gave to the disciples. Ordinary fishermen spoke boldly before the Jewish Supreme Court about Jesus as the only source of salvation. How? They were "filled with the Holy Spirit" (Acts 4:8).

The gift of languages is repeated with some variation three times in Acts. The first time was on the day of Pentecost. The second was in Cornelius' house, as the Spirit came on a Gentile God-fearer (see Acts 10:45-46). The third time was in Ephesus among a dozen people who had heard only about John the Baptist but not about Jesus and the Holy Spirit (see Acts 19:1-7).

The common denominator in all three of these episodes was the crossing of an ethnic boundary. On the day of Pentecost, the Spirit came on Jews, particularly those from outside Jerusalem (see Acts 2). With Cornelius and his household, the gospel crossed over to God-fearing Gentiles.

The conversion of the small group in Ephesus marks the extension of the gospel to those Gentiles who had not yet become God-fearers. They were pure Gentiles, which is to say that to some, they were completely impure. Because of the significance of the transitions from Jew to God-fearer to Gentile, the Holy Spirit marked the occasion with this specific miracle, emphasizing the personal nature of God and the trans-cultural character of the gospel.

The Spirit not only empowered the mission, He guided it. At crucial moments, He directed the church or its leaders to take a particular action. At times He told them to go to a particular location; more than once He slammed a door closed, preventing ministry in a certain area. The Spirit was like a general, executing the strategy that would best accomplish the spreading of the gospel.

This divine general was also very interested in selecting others to serve on His staff. He included the eleven disciples Jesus had chosen. (The twelfth, Judas, had committed suicide after realizing what he had done to Jesus). The early church felt it was important to replace Judas. They nominated two men who had followed Jesus from the beginning and who had been eyewitnesses of the Lord's resurrection.

They chose between the two by casting lots—basically, dice—to decide on Judas' replacement. While this might seem strange to us, it illustrates perfectly how much the early Christians depended on the Holy Spirit make the final decision.

The best-known of the staff selected by the Spirit was Saul of Tarsus. Yes, you heard me right, the very same Saul who had been maniacally persecuting the Christians was tapped by the Spirit to advance the church. I'll say more about him shortly.

The establishment of the church

One of the Spirit's most powerful acts was the creation of the church. You might not think of the church as powerful, but looks can be deceiving. The church—not the building or the organization, but the spiritual fellowship of believers gathered to worship and scattered to serve—represents a living example of God's plan at work.

Wherever the apostles preached the gospel and people responded, a church was formed. The believers met together to sing praises, pray (including the Lord's Prayer), read the Bible (our Old Testament) and have someone explain it. They might also read a letter containing wise counsel written by a church leader; these letters circulated from church to church. Those gathered would take communion (also known as the Lord's Supper and the Eucharist) in obedience to Jesus' command to eat this meal in His memory.

These gatherings, held each Sunday in honor of Christ's resurrection, were more than a time to remember Christ. They were also times to gather in the presence of the Spirit. He was the audience who heard their prayers and praises. He not only inspired the Word of Scripture, but also delivered messages—prophecies—through individuals in the congregation. The church, said one early Christian leader, is "where the Spirit flourishes."

These local congregations, filled with people in various stages of spiritual maturity, were the means by which God intended to accomplish His plan. They would provide the nurturing atmosphere in which the Holy Spirit could produce spiritual maturity. He was the gardener, the individual believer was the plant, and the church was the greenhouse.

These greenhouses are what you might call "sanctifying contexts." Sanctification is another word for the process by which God saves us, that is, by which He produces reconciliation in all of our relationships. We can say two things for sure about sanctification: this is the work of the Holy Spirit (see 2 Thessalonian 2:13), and it happens in a community, the ideal community being the local church.

The Spirit is the one who enables us to be reconciled to God. He brings us back to life from our spiritual death (see 2 Corinthians 3:6; Titus 3:5) and lives inside of us (see Romans 8:9; Ephesians 5:18). Communication helps strengthen any relationship, which is why the Spirit helps us when we pray (see Romans 8:26-27).

One result of having our relationship with God restored is that our nature can be changed to resemble Christ's. The Apostle Paul compares this to producing fruit like love, joy and peace. And who is the gardener? You guessed it, the Holy Spirit (see Galatians 5:22-23).

Earlier in this chapter we noted that the gospel went out first among the Jews and then to the Gentiles. These two groups did not naturally get along. Jews regarded Gentiles as unclean because they didn't observe the dietary laws and weren't circumcised. Gentiles regarded Jewish laws as unnecessary and Judaism as too concerned about things that don't matter.

Tensions finally reached the point that the church leadership needed to address the matter. A conference was called in Jerusalem (see Acts 15), where the leaders heard testimony from the Apostle Paul and from those who felt Paul was too lax in allowing Gentile converts into the church. The Apostle Peter spoke as well, reminding everyone of his ministry to Cornelius, the Gentile God-fearer.

Finally, the church heard from James, Jesus' brother and a man highly regarded for his adherence to Jewish laws. He pointed out how the examples of Peter and Paul agreed with the Old Testament prophets who promised God would make a place among His people for the Gentiles (see Acts 15:16-18).

Paul, the apostle to the Gentiles

While the central character in the Book of Acts is God's Spirit, the central human figure is Saul of Tarsus. We know him better as

Paul; his parents likely gave him both names, Saul to reflect his Jewishness and Paul his Roman heritage.

Saul was born and spent his early years in the city of Tarsus. He moved to Jerusalem as a boy to study under the great Rabbi Gamaliel. Saul devoted himself to the sect of Judaism known as the Pharisees (see Philippians 3:4-6) and viciously persecuted the Christians (see Acts 8:1-3; 22:4; 26:10).

While on his way to Damascus to ferret out Christians, Saul experienced a dramatic visionary confrontation by Jesus. It left him physically blinded but spiritually enlightened. To call it a conversion is not quite accurate; the better term for Paul's change might be completion or realization. When he saw the risen Christ, he realized that Jesus was who the Christians said he was, the Messiah.

At that moment on the road to Damascus, Paul understood that Jesus was the key to God's plan of reconciliation. This realization made sense of the puzzle. As a Pharisee, Saul believed that the law of Moses was God's fullest revelation of Himself. Now he realized that the law was meant to prepare the way for Jesus the Messiah, God in human form.

The story of Saul's transformation from Christian killer to apostle to the Gentiles (see Galatians 1:16; Romans 15:16; Ephesians 3:8) is compelling; it is recounted two more times in the Book of Acts. But it doesn't explain why God chose Paul in the first place.

Of course, it helps that the church's missionary-in-chief could point to a dramatic encounter with the risen Christ. Paul probably needed this experience to anchor his confidence in the face of tremendous opposition. His experience would have been helpful in leading other Jews to Christ.

But why give this experience to Paul and not someone else?

It's probably safe to say that there was no one else with Paul's unique blend of personality, intellect, and preparation. He had just what would be required of the man who would explain God's plan, not only to his contemporaries, but to Christians throughout the world and across the ages through his writings, which constitute a huge chunk of the New Testament.

His training under Gamaliel, one of the leading rabbis within Judaism, prepared him with a thorough understanding of the Scriptures. This training also sharpened his intellect to the point of brilliance (see Acts 26:24; 2 Peter 3:16). He knew Greek philosophy and could quote pagan poets from memory. We know he spoke at least two languages—Greek and Aramaic; he likely knew other languages as well.

All of this enabled Paul to explain God's plan as fulfilled in Christ and transmit it in writing. These writings informed his contemporaries, both Jews who had some familiarity with the Old Testament, and Gentiles, some of whom knew the Scriptures, but others who did not. Thanks to "professor" Paul, they came to understand God's heart for the world. Not only his contemporaries, but all Christians everywhere at all times, have been Paul's students.

Paul was chosen, not only for his intellect, but also for his personality and character. God gave him the task of explaining the gospel, but also proclaiming it. He wasn't just professor Paul, he was also preacher Paul.

Once commissioned by God as a missionary, Paul didn't stop. He traveled widely and endured unbelievable difficulties (see 2 Corinthians 11:23-29) without complaint. For a time, he even worked to support himself while he ministered (see Acts 20:34; 1 Thessalonians 2:9). His strong personality led him to criticize his opponents (see Galatians 5:12), the Jewish high priest (see Acts

23:3), and even the Apostle Peter (see Galatians 2:11-21). Yet Paul could also be gentle when necessary (see 1 Corinthians 9:19-22; Acts 20:7-12; Philippians 2:25-30).

Paul wasn't chosen for his physical strength. In fact, he had what appears to have been a debilitating chronic illness. He speaks of it as a "thorn in my flesh" (2 Corinthians 12:7). This has been variously understood as a type of eye disease, epilepsy, malaria, or migraine headaches.

Several times Paul prayed that this malady would be removed. He recognized that without this limitation he could do still more for God. God said no, pointing out that Paul's weakness was to become a source of strength. Paul agreed: "When I am weak, then I am strong" (2 Corinthians 12:10).

God chose Paul, not in spite of this handicap, but with it. He wanted Paul to illustrate a truth we have learned before in God's classroom, from childless Abraham and Sarah, from the Israelites before the Egyptians, from David before Goliath, and from Joseph before the Pharaoh; God's strength is perfected in weakness, if the weak will walk by faith.

But why appoint Paul as apostle to the Gentiles? Why not Peter? After all, Peter was one of the original disciples, one of Jesus' inner circle, and the first to cross the Jew-Gentile barrier.

Paul was chosen for what he represented. God had promised that the Jews, Abraham's descendants, would be a blessing to the nations. What better way to emphasize this point than by taking a Jew—the most Jewish Jew you ever knew, giving him an unforgettable encounter with the central figure in God's plan, transforming him by the Spirit, and sending him to preach the good news to the Gentiles. A closer look at the gospel as explained by Paul is where we turn next as we explore the big picture of the Bible.

Study Questions

1. How have you seen the Holy Spirit at work in your life?

2. If the church is so powerful, why does it often seem so weak?

3. How does your church provide a sanctifying context to help people experience the fullness of reconciliation in their relationships with God, others, self, and nature?

4. What does it mean to you that "God's strength is perfected in weakness, if the weak will walk by faith"?

Chapter Fourteen

GOD'S PLAN EXPLAINED

The New Testament Epistles

Introduction

Having explored how the gospel spread in the decades immediately following Jesus' ascension, let's turn to the letters that make up so much of the New Testament. Jesus had assured His disciples that after He left, He would send His Spirit who would help them understand what He had taught them. The epistles reveal what the Spirit taught them; they show how Jesus kept His promise.

Epistles are letters written by church leaders, usually apostles. The earliest may have been the Book of James, written by Jesus' brother within a decade of the resurrection. The latest were probably the three short letters written by the Apostle John. Paul wrote most of the letters, usually to specific churches or individuals.

Each of these letters was written for a reason or reasons. There may have been a problem that the author intended to correct (for example, 1 Corinthians 1-6) or something positive to be commended (for example, Philippians). The congregation may have asked a question that the letter seeks to answer (see 1 Corinthians 7-8). Sometimes the letter writer wanted something from the congregation. Paul wrote to the Romans, in part, so they would support his missionary journey to Spain (see Romans 15:23-29).

The Spirit often provided His teaching in response to the questions and struggles faced by the early Christians. For example, the Christians' claim that Jesus was equal to God brought them into conflict with Jews and non-Jews, conflict that raised further questions. Through these epistles, the Spirit provided further insight into Jesus' divinity.

While very helpful to the first-century churches, these letters include lots of cultural and historical particularities unique to that time and place, such as the role of women in Roman culture and whether to eat meat sacrificed to idols. Because the Holy Spirit inspired these letters, they contain the right response for that culture for those issues. They also provide more general insights that we can apply to all cultures and issues.

This combination of what mattered for a particular culture and what matters for all cultures makes interpreting the epistles a little tricky. It's not like we're given a bullet-list of "Ten Timeless Teachings for Running a Church." The Spirit inspired the letter's author to provide the proper answers to specific issues, while also demonstrating how versatile and practical the gospel can be, and while providing eternal truths still applicable today.

Most of these letters were addressed to churches. Even those sent to individuals had the church as a secondary audience (see Philemon 1:1-2). The way these letters transmit and preserve the development of the gospel highlights the importance of the church, a topic we'll return to later in this chapter.

The development of the gospel

Jesus' divinity

Although the letters address many different questions, certain themes stand out, themes that develop our understanding of the gospel. One such theme was Christ's divine nature. In the gospels, Jesus claimed to be equal with God. The epistles contain the Spirit's clarification of what it means that Jesus is fully divine.

Although all the New Testament epistles make this point, for some Christ's divinity figures prominently in their message. The Book of Hebrews begins by asserting that Jesus is God's appointed heir and maker of everything. He is "the radiance of God's glory and the exact representation of his being, sustaining all things by his powerful word" (Hebrews 1:3).

To say that Jesus is the "radiance of God's glory" is like comparing God to the sun and Jesus to the sunbeams; you can't distinguish between them. Calling him "the exact representation of his [God's] being," refers to the complete similarity between the image on a coin and the die from which that coin was stamped. When the writer of Hebrews describes Christ as "sustaining all things," he attributes to Jesus what the Old Testament attributed to God (for example, see Psalm 104).

In his letter to the Colossians, the Apostle Paul spoke of Jesus as "the image of the invisible God" (1:15). He not only created all things; they were created for Him (1:16). "For God was pleased to have all his fullness dwell in him, and through him to reconcile to himself all things, whether things on earth or things in heaven, by making peace through his blood, shed on the cross" (1:19-20; see also 2:9-10). Because Jesus was fully God, He was able to make "peace through his blood" (1:20), peace between humanity and God, each other, self, and the natural world.

One of the most powerful passages describing Christ's divinity is found in Paul's letter to the Church at Philippi:

> [5] In your relationships with one another, have the same mindset as Christ Jesus: [6] Who, being in very nature God, did not consider equality with God something to be used to his own advantage; [7] rather, he made himself nothing by taking the very nature of a servant, being made in human likeness. [8] And being found in appearance as a man, he

humbled himself by becoming obedient to death—even death on a cross! [9] Therefore God exalted him to the highest place and gave him the name that is above every name, [10] that at the name of Jesus every knee should bow, in heaven and on earth and under the earth, [11] and every tongue acknowledge that Jesus Christ is Lord, to the glory of God the Father (Philippians 2:5-11).

Paul asserts Jesus' divinity ("in very nature God"), but then speaks of Jesus' decision to become human ("made himself nothing"). This helps us better understand what happened in the incarnation. Jesus wasn't just a human being who had a special relationship with God, He was God Himself who became a human.

And why? So that He could die on the cross (see verse 8; see Colossians 1:20). Obviously, the Christian's claim that Jesus was actually God seems to be contradicted by His death as a common criminal; it sounds like foolishness (see 1 Corinthians 1:18). Even worse, the Jews believed that anyone who died on the cross was actually accursed (see 1 Corinthians 1:23; Galatians 3:13; Deuteronomy 21:23).

The Spirit helped the early Christians to see Jesus' death on the cross, not as something to be ashamed of, but as something to proudly proclaim. Rather than the ultimate example of weakness, the cross was a great source of power. By it, God forgave our sins and "having disarmed the powers and authorities, he made a public spectacle of them, triumphing over them by the cross" (Colossians 2:15). Instead of something to be ashamed of, the cross shamed the spiritual forces that opposed God. As a result, Paul would not boast in anything "except in the cross of our Lord Jesus Christ" (Galatians 6:14).

The extended quotation above explains that Christ didn't just die and stay dead, He also rose from the dead. Or as Paul put it, God "exalted him to the highest place" (Philippians 2:9). The resurrection was one of the central tenets in the preaching of the early church. They understood it was essential for the Christian life that Christ be raised from the dead.

We have seen that Christ's resurrection was God's stamp of approval on Jesus' life of faith, the stamp of approval that allowed the early church to understand God's redemptive plan and Christ's central role in it. Jesus' resurrection was also an essential component of our salvation. "He [Christ] was delivered over to death for our sins and was raised to life for our justification" (Romans 4:25).

Because Christ rose from the dead, Christians also have the hope of rising from the dead. As Paul explained to the Corinthians, "Christ has indeed been raised from the dead, the firstfruits of those who have fallen asleep" (1 Corinthians 15:20).

Christ's resurrection provides us with the power, not only to one day rise from death, but to live our lives now through the Spirit. "We were therefore buried with him through baptism into death in order that, just as Christ was raised from the dead through the glory of the Father, we too may live a new life" (Romans 6:4).

The Church

Thanks to the Holy Spirit's inspiration, we also learn more about the church. The epistles provide many metaphors that describe the church, such as ship, temple, household, family, flock, and army. Perhaps the best known is the comparison of the church to Christ's body.

Paul used this metaphor in many of his letters. Sometimes he used it to teach how the church can and must be unified, even though diverse. It's like the human body, explained Paul, with different parts all working together (see Romans 12:5; 1 Corinthians 12; Ephesians 4:12).

At other times, Paul used this metaphor to make it clear that the church is the body of which Christ is the head. The church isn't a democracy; it's a body that takes instruction from the head (Colossians 2:18-19). Paul also referred to Christ as head of the body to illustrate the significance of the church (see Ephesians 1:22-23). We are God's masterpiece, put on display to demonstrate the gospel's power to reconcile humans to God and every other relationship (see Ephesians 2:6-7).

As we've seen, the church began among Jews, but soon came to include Gentiles as well. In response to the resulting tension, Paul turned again to the body metaphor. He describes how Jesus, through His death on the cross, brought together these two groups and created "one new humanity out of the two, thus making peace" (Ephesians 2:15; see 3:6). Now "there is neither Jew nor Gentile, . . . for you are all one in Christ Jesus" (Galatians 3:28).

The nature and work of the Spirit of God

Through the epistles, the Spirit also helps us better understand His own nature and work. We learned a lot about the Holy Spirit from the Book of Acts, how He empowered the Christians at Pentecost, filled them with courage in the face of opposition, enabled them to do miracles, and guided them in their mission. The Book of Acts reveals the Spirit as the central figure in the establishment of the church.

In the New Testament letters, we see the Holy Spirit's activity in Christian worship, empowering people to carry out the full spectrum of ministry (see 1 Corinthians 12, 14). He lives among God's people, making them a living temple (1 Corinthians 3:16).

He not only inhabits the church, the Spirit also lives within each person who is part of the church (see 1 Corinthians 6:19). God puts His Spirit into our hearts to make us more like God. Paul describes this as producing the fruit of the Spirit (see Galatians 5:22-23). The indwelling Spirit also confirms that the believer is a true child of God (see Romans 8:15; Galatians 4:6; 1 John 4:13).

One of God's most prominent roles in the Old Testament was teacher, instructing His people in preparation for Christ's coming. Jesus had told us to expect the Spirit to teach (see John 16:13); the letters provide a look into the Spirit's classroom. As Paul wrote to the Corinthian church, "This is what we speak, not in words taught us by human wisdom but in words taught by the Spirit, explaining spiritual realities with Spirit-taught words" (1 Corinthians 2:13).

Reconciliation

Up to this point in the chapter we've ranged widely throughout the epistles to identify how the Spirit was developing the gospel. Now let's walk through one of these letters, Romans, to watch the Spirit reveal how the gospel begins to bring reconciliation to all our broken relationships.

Reconciliation with God

"Therefore, since we have been justified through faith, we have peace with God through our Lord Jesus Christ" (Romans 5:1). Although separated from God by sin, Paul makes clear in this letter that Christians have been graciously reunited with God because of what Jesus did on the cross.

Paul doesn't pull any punches; everyone has sinned and deserves death, a point he makes clearly in the first three chapters of Romans. This includes the Jews, who thought they were acceptable because they were God's chosen people and had the law of Moses. Paul has both Jews and Gentiles in mind when he announces, "all have sinned and fall short of the glory of God" (Romans 3:23).

Yes, the Jews were privileged to receive the law, but they had not kept its commandments. So they're no different from the Gentiles who also had a law—the law of conscience—which they broke. All of us are lawbreakers.

God never intended us to reconcile ourselves to Him by obeying the law. We were always meant to be reconciled by faith. "But now apart from the law the righteousness of God has been made known, to which the Law and the Prophets testify. This righteousness is given through faith in Jesus Christ to all who believe" (Romans 3:21-22).

When Paul says we are saved by faith, he means we've accepted God's gift of salvation. We acknowledge that what Jesus did on the cross and empty tomb was sufficient for the forgiveness of our sins and our reconciliation with God.

We do not need to offer additional sacrifices to satisfy God's justice. In fact, if we try, we end up doing more harm than good. Christ has offered Himself as the once-and-for all sacrifice (see Hebrews 10). Now any other sacrifices, in the words of one writer, are not only dead, but deadly. In trying to earn God's favor, we end up forfeiting access to God's grace.

When Paul speaks of salvation by faith, he also means we are saved by our faith because of Jesus' faith. Because Jesus trusted God to the end, the very moment of death, God accepted His self-sacrifice as the price for our salvation. We are saved by faith in Christ because of the faith of Christ.

Someone might ask, "When did God change His mind and decide to save people by faith instead of by works?" Actually, salvation has always been by faith and never by works. The law was never intended to bring salvation but to help the saved know how to live.

Paul makes this point by pointing to Abraham (see Romans 4). God had commanded Abraham to become circumcised (see Genesis 17). Circumcision was an essential aspect of what would become the law of Moses and the distinguishing mark of being a Jew. But Paul points out that the command to be circumcised came *after* Abraham had already trusted in God by faith (see Genesis 15). Faith came first, then came the law.

One could think that now that Christ has come, the law has been set aside. After all, it was only a work-around. Sacrifices for sin are now deadly, not only for the animals but also for those who offer them. Paul specifically warns against trying to be made right with God by keeping the law (Romans 4:4-6; 9:31; 10:5; Galatians 2:16-21; 3:2-13).

Surprisingly, Paul asserts that the law remains in effect, not the law of Moses but the "law that requires faith" (Romans 3:27). Careless readers of Paul have concluded that he rejects the law in favor of grace, often quoting "you are not under the law, but under grace" (Romans 6:14).

Look more closely and you see that Paul is speaking of two laws, the law of works and the law of faith. Or, as he describes them in Romans 8:2, the "law of sin and death" and "the law of the Spirit who gives life." He soundly rejects the law of works but celebrates the law of life (see Romans 3:31; 8:2, 4, 7; 10:4; 13:8, 10).

The law of life is the same law of love for God and neighbor that Christ invoked (see Matthew 22:35-40). Elsewhere Paul will refer to this as the Law of Christ (Galatians 5:14; 6:2), a law that will never be revoked.

Salvation not only involves being justified, that is, made righteous in God's sight by the forgiveness of our sins. It also means that God gives us the Holy Spirit who allows us to live in fellowship with God (see Romans 8:1-17). We are not only *pronounced* righteous, God revives the moral image so we can *become* righteous by the power of the Spirit. Both are necessary if we are to enjoy fellowship with God.

Reconciliation with others

Those who live in harmony with God will live in harmony with others. They will "be devoted to one another in love" (Romans 12:10), put the needs of others above their own, and be generous and hospitable. They will even love their enemies and never take revenge (see Romans 12:1-21).

This should be especially true within the church. Unfortunately, the early Christians were no better at loving others than are Christians today. Hence, Paul spent a considerable portion of his letters calling for unity.

On the one hand, Paul's expectation that Christians would love each other seems preposterous. After all, you have congregations made up of Jews and Gentiles, each side raised to dislike the other. You have great diversity in social class, with slaves and slave owners worshiping in the same congregation.

You have women and men worshiping together. We might take this for granted today but it created no little tension at that time. Paul might preach that "there is neither Jew nor Gentile, neither slave nor free, nor is there male and female, for you are all one in Christ Jesus" (Galatians 3:28), but it seems too much to ask that such a diverse group should actually get along.

Yet Paul not only called for this, he insisted on it. Unity wasn't just a way to keep the church growing, it was essential evidence that the gospel was working. Inter-personal strife resulted from sin; inter-personal harmony was a *necessary* result of salvation.

Paul had to address this among the Christians in Rome. This congregation saw division along ethnic lines, Jew against Gentile. In addition, the two sides had theological differences. The effect: a church divided.

The antidote: love. Paul appealed to both sides to please their neighbors "for their good, to build them up," using Christ as an example (Romans 15:2-3). They were to "accept one another" as they had been accepted by Christ, "in order to bring praise to God" (Romans 15:7). By showing love in spite of their differences, God would get the glory, for it was God who had made possible this self-sacrificing love.

Reconciliation with self

Sin also produced intra-personal alienation, evidenced by a pervasive sense of shame and fear. Salvation heals this alienation, giving us peace within ourselves. Paul displays what this healing looks like in Romans 7-8.

In Romans 7, Paul describes an individual in turmoil, a "wretched man" (Romans 7:24). Although Paul uses first-person language (I, me), he isn't describing his own experience. Perhaps he felt this way before he encountered Christ, or perhaps he is speaking rhetorically.

Either way, this cannot be Paul's present experience. How could the man in Romans 7 be the same person who tells the Corinthians to "Follow my example, as I follow the example of Christ" (1 Corinthians 11:1). How could the "wretched man" in Romans 7 be the same one who tells the Philippians to "Join together in following my example, . . . and just as you have us as a model, keep your eyes on those who live as we do" (Philippians

3:17) and who commands them to put into practice whatever they've seen in him (see Philippians 4:9; see also 2 Timothy 1:13).

In Paul's description of this "wretched man," we see a person living at war with himself. This person can't understand his own actions over which he seems to have no control. Filled with shame, he seems afraid, even of himself.

But there is hope for this man. In Romans 8, Paul announces that through Christ we can now be free of condemnation, free from the law of sin and death, free to live in the power of the Spirit (see Romans 8:1-2). "The mind governed by the flesh is death, but the mind governed by the Spirit is life and peace" (Romans 8:6).

Through the Spirit, we can find victory over shame and fear. God has spoken truth into our hearts and with that truth we can counter the lies we've been listening to. Life in the Spirit means living according to God's expectations, not those we unwisely place on ourselves, nor those placed on us by others. God offers us peace within ourselves, a peace "that transcends all understanding" (Philippians 4:7).

Reconciliation with nature

Salvation not only brings reconciliation with God, others, and self, it also restores the relationship God intended us to have with creation. What God begins in this life for this and the other three relationships, He will complete in the consummating moment (more on this in our next chapter).

One of the consequences of alienation from nature is suffering. We saw it with Adam and Eve in the Garden, and have seen it ever since. The gospel transforms suffering. By willingly embracing suffering on the cross, Jesus removed its destructive power. Now no amount of suffering can "separate us from the love of God that is in Christ Jesus our Lord" (Romans 8:35-39). In fact, suffering can actually bring us closer to God (see Romans 8:17; 1 Peter 2:20).

Paul looks ahead to the day when God will completely remove suffering, and every other effect of the curse on creation.

> I consider that our present sufferings are not worth comparing with the glory that will be revealed in us. For the creation waits in eager expectation for the children of God to be revealed. For the creation was subjected to frustration, not by its own choice, but by the will of the one who subjected it, in hope that the creation itself will be liberated from its bondage to decay and brought into the freedom and glory of the children of God. We know that the whole creation has been groaning as in the pains of childbirth right up to the present time. Not only so, but we ourselves, who have the firstfruits of the Spirit, groan inwardly as we wait eagerly for our adoption to sonship, the redemption of our bodies. For in this hope we were saved. But hope that is seen is no hope at all. Who hopes for what they already have? But if we hope for what we do not yet have, we wait for it patiently (Romans 8:18-25).

What Paul describes here in such an abbreviated way, we see more fully displayed in the last book of the New Testament. There we find Christ making "everything new" (Revelation 21:5). That book is the final stop in our fly-over of the Bible.

Study Questions

1. Spend time meditating on what the epistles say about Jesus (e.g. Hebrews 1:2-3; Philippians 2:6-11; Colossians 1:15-23). Write out a prayer expressing thanks and praise to Jesus Christ.

2. Using a study Bible or Bible dictionary, look up other passages that talk about the church. Make a list of all the metaphors used to describe the church and reflect on what each tells us about the church.

3. One big struggle for the early church was bringing together Jews and Gentiles into one body. What is a significant struggle within the church today? How might God want to help us overcome this?

4. Review the passages provided here which speak of reconciliation (with God, others, self, nature) in Romans. Reflect on each passage and write down your thoughts. Add other scriptures that deal with reconciliation.

Chapter Fifteen

GOD'S PLAN FULFILLED

The Book of Revelation

Introduction

The last book of the Bible may be the least appreciated. I admit, it is a puzzling book, filled with angels and dragons, and singing, lots and lots of singing.

Many have devoted themselves to understanding its visions; some of these interpreters are convinced they have succeeded. They're quite sure they know the secrets of the book and are only too ready to proclaim their insights to others. The fact that their "obvious" conclusions don't agree with the obvious conclusions of others doesn't seem to temper their enthusiasm.

Unfortunately, this combination of difficulty and controversy has prompted many Christians to take a hands-off approach to the Book of Revelation. Unfortunate indeed because this is the only book in the Bible that contains a blessing on those who read it, those who hear it, and those who take it to heart (see Revelation 1:3). To neglect the Book of Revelation is to miss out on a great blessing.

Some view the book as primarily describing events that occurred among the early Christians; for others, the book describes events that will unfold only in the last days. Some interpret the book as primarily symbolic, except for those passages that should be taken literally; others begin with the opposite assumption, that the book should be interpreted literally except for those passages that should be taken symbolically.

Regardless of one's preferred interpretation, everyone can agree that this book pictures how God brings ultimate reconciliation to all four of the relationships broken by sin. In the final vision there are no more work-arounds, only eternal solutions. What a blessing to learn that we have experienced partial reconciliation already and total reconciliation is coming!

All the book's interpreters would also agree that the Book of Revelation was written, at least in part, to call the church to be a faithful witness in the face of persecution. God reveals the conclusion of His plan, not for our entertainment, but so that we can carry out our role as faithful witnesses in our day, blessed to give our lives for the sake of the gospel.

Another point on which all interpreters will certainly agree is the centrality of Jesus. We see this in the book's opening words: "The revelation from Jesus Christ" (1:1). Jesus is the One who reveals the contents of the book, but He is also the One revealed, the central character in its chapters.

Among the portraits of Jesus on display in the gallery of Revelation, we'll examine three: Jesus as the fulfillment of God's plan, Jesus as King of kings, and Jesus as the unfolder of human destiny.

Jesus as the fulfillment of God's plan

In chapter 11, in our consideration of the gospels, we drew attention to the fact that Jesus is the central figure in God's plan, the picture on the box that makes sense of the puzzle pieces. Everything in the Old Testament pointed forward to Jesus; the books that followed describe the implications of His life and work.

After the gospels, no part of the Bible makes Jesus more central than the Book of Revelation. We are shown who Jesus truly is.

The gospels revealed his human nature and gave us a glimpse of his divine nature. In the Book of Revelation His divine nature is on full view, without allowing us to lose sight of his humanity.

One way we see Christ's divinity is when the Book of Revelation ascribes to Jesus a title that elsewhere it gives to God the Father. In Revelation 1:8, God describes Himself as "the Alpha and the Omega." These are the first and last letters of the Greek alphabet; the phrase implies the origin and destiny of all things. God the Father repeats this phrase in Revelation 21:6, again applying it to Himself.

Just one chapter later, in Revelation 22:13, Jesus uses this term to describe Himself: "I am the Alpha and the Omega, the First and the Last, the Beginning and the End." The implication is clear: Although distinct, Jesus and God are one in essence.

The opening vision of Jesus borrows imagery from the Old Testament to portray Christ as God (see Revelation 1:12-16). Not only is Christ pictured with glowing feet and powerful voice, He holds stars in His hand, a sword proceeds from His mouth, and His face shines like the sun. Even some of the descriptive phrases used here—hair like wool and white as snow, a figure surrounded by flames—are used to picture God in Daniel 7:9-10.

We are shown Jesus' divinity as we stand in God's throne room in heaven (Revelation 4-5). As the scene opens, we see God seated on His throne, with heavenly beings extoling His greatness in song. Then Christ appears, standing in the center of the throne (Revelation 5:6). By the time this chapter ends, the heavenly beings are singing praises "to him who sits on the throne and to the Lamb" (Revelation 5:13). We saw glimpses of Christ's divine nature in the gospels; the epistles expanded our understanding of what this meant. The Book of Revelation makes it very clear that Jesus is the "Son of God" (2:18).

Yet we are never far in Revelation from Jesus' humanity. Early on He is called "the faithful witness" (1:5), a reference to His life of obedient testimony to the Father. Some even see in Revelation 12 the story of Christ's birth. A woman gives "birth to a son, a male child, 'who will rule all the nations with an iron scepter'" (Revelation 12:5).

But the term translated "witness" in Revelation 1:5 can also be translated as martyr. The Book of Revelation affirms that Jesus not only lived a life of obedient testimony, He also died as a martyr in obedience to God.

We saw in the epistles how the cross became, for Christians, a sign of power and hope. This theme continues in the Book of Revelation. While emphasizing Christ's divinity it also emphasizes His sacrificial death.

We are still in the opening verses of the book when we hear that Christ "loves us and has freed us from our sins by his blood" (Revelation 1:5). In the throne room, the heavenly beings praise Christ as the Lamb who was slain (Revelation 5:6, 9, 12). Christians are able to triumph over our enemy "by the blood of the Lamb and by the word of their testimony" (Revelation 12:11).

Just as the Book of Revelation never loses sight of Christ's sacrificial death, it continually reminds us of His resurrection. Jesus is called "the firstborn from the dead" (Revelation 1:5). He introduces Himself to John, the author of Revelation, with these words: "Do not be afraid. I am the First and the Last. I am the Living One; I was dead, and now look, I am alive for ever and ever! And I hold the keys of death and Hades" (Revelation 1:17b-18).

Jesus as King

The Book of Revelation begins by referring to Jesus as "the faithful witness" and "firstborn from the dead." It also opens by calling Him the "ruler of the kings of the earth" (Revelation 1:5). Near the end it pictures Him as the "King of Kings and Lord of Lords" (Revelation 19:16).

Throughout the Old Testament, God revealed Himself as King. Like a wise chief, He ruled over His people, Israel. But by virtue of having created everything, God was also ruler over the whole earth (see Psalm 47:7-8; 86:8-10; 96:10; 99:2; 138:4-5).

With the introduction of the monarchy, we saw that God was willing to rule through a person, Israel's king. Later, prophets anticipated a king from David's line, an anointed one, a Messiah. The Jews took this hope with them into exile and nurtured it through their season of subjugation under foreign captors.

This is one reason they responded so enthusiastically to the announcement of Jesus' arrival. Here was a descendant of David with royal aspirations. His entry into Jerusalem on Palm Sunday was the moment they had been waiting for. But when they realized Jesus was not the king they expected, their enthusiasm turned to murderous hatred. The "King of the Jews" hung in shame on a Roman cross.

The resurrection of Jesus and coming of the Holy Spirit showed the early Christians that Christ was King, just not the king many expected. The cross was not the punishment for failure to assert His rule; the cross and subsequent resurrection were the path to ascend His throne (see Ephesians 1:19-22; 1 Peter 3:21-22; Hebrews 1:8).

Remember how Paul described it:

> And being found in appearance as a man, he [Jesus] humbled himself by becoming obedient to death—even death on a cross! Therefore God exalted him to the highest place and gave him the name that is above every name, that at

the name of Jesus every knee should bow, in heaven and on earth and under the earth, and every tongue acknowledge that Jesus Christ is Lord, to the glory of God the Father (Philippians 2:8-11).

The Old Testament anticipated Christ's reign, the gospels announced it, and the epistles explained it. But more than any other book, Revelation *displays* Christ in His role as King.

The "ruler of the kings of the earth" (Revelation 1:5) speaks with authority to the seven churches (see Revelation 2-3). His words not only demonstrate His sovereignty over the church, but over the world that was persecuting the church.

Christ takes His rightful place at the center of God's throne (see Revelation 5:6) and in the praises of the heavenly worshipers (see Revelation 5:9-13). He demonstrates His sovereignty by opening the scroll, the only one worthy to do so (see Revelation 6-8).

At the heart of this book we find its central truth: "The kingdom of this world has become the kingdom of our Lord and of his Messiah, and he will reign for ever and ever" (Revelation 11:15). After a series of visions that describe the rise of those forces opposed to God, we read of their shattering defeat at the hands of Christ: "They will wage war against the Lamb, but the Lamb will triumph over them because he is the Lord of lords and King of kings" (Revelation 17:14).

Just before the great final battle, we see the armies of heaven "riding on white horses and dressed in fine linen, white and clean" (Revelation 19:14). At their head rides the One known as "Faithful and True" and "the Word of God." His eyes blaze, his head crowned with many crowns, a sharp sword comes from His mouth "with which to strike down the nations" (see Revelation 19:11-15). Written on His robe are these words: "King of Kings and Lord of Lords" (Revelation 19:16). Victory is assured!

Jesus as unfolder of history

The scene in God's throne room (see Revelation 4-5) occupies a key moment in the book. It reveals that this revelation is primarily about Jesus, the One who shares a place on God's throne.

It also reminds us that God remains in control. Human leaders may rise up against His people and even persecute them, but God is on His throne. He has a plan and will bring that plan to completion in the proper time.

The throne room scene also highlights a scroll sealed with seven seals. This scroll represents God's future plan for the world. As it is unsealed and unrolled, the final stage of that plan goes into effect.

But who has the authority to break the seals and open the scroll? To do so would require one who stands outside of history, yet whose actions within history have qualified Him for this moment.

Only One is worthy, the Lion of Judah who is also the slain but living Lamb, Jesus. Only He is worthy to take the scroll and break the seals. The One who was the plan's centerpiece is the only One who can bring that plan to fruition.

The unfolding of God's plan occupies most of the rest of the Book of Revelation. We see the breaking of the seven seals in chapters 6-8; the breaking of the seventh triggers the sounding of seven trumpets (see Revelation 8-11). The blast of the seventh trumpet triggers a series of visions, including the pouring out of seven bowls (see Revelation 11-18). With the pouring out of the seventh bowl comes the final act of judgment (see Revelation 16:17-18), the destruction of "Babylon," the city that represents those who oppose God.

Interpretations vary widely about when and how this happens. Some see it describing in heavily symbolic language the struggle that took place between the early Church and Rome. Others consider these visions of things to come, using language that is mostly literal. Still others combine these views in one way or another.

All interpreters agree that the Church will face struggle and persecution, even martyrdom. In the face of such danger, Christians must remain faithful, they must overcome "by the blood of the Lamb and by the word of their testimony" (Revelation 12:11). Every interpreter also agrees that, in the end, Christ wins. He defeats all His enemies and most importantly, finally and forever conquers hell, death and the Devil.

In the closing two chapters of the Book of Revelation we see the consummation of God's plan of reconciliation. Much earlier, sin had entered the Garden, bringing humanity and nature under a curse. God inaugurated a plan to break that curse, a plan focused on Jesus.

Now, in the New Jerusalem, we hear the long-awaited announcement: "No longer will there be any curse" (Revelation 22:3a). The "old order of things has passed away" (Revelation 21:4), and God is "making everything new!" (Revelation 21:5).

Reconciliation with God

With the curse broken, we can now experience complete reconciliation with God. Humans have known partial reconciliation, such as occurred in the tabernacle and temple. Through the gospel, the Holy Spirit provided a foretaste of full reconciliation, but now the moment has finally arrived. A loud voice announces from God's throne, "Look! God's dwelling place is now among the people, and he will dwell with them. They will be his people, and God himself will be with them and be their God." We will serve Him and all "will see his face" (Revelation 22:3-4).

I love the picture of God wiping every tear from our eyes (see Revelation 21:4a). Like a loving father, He draws near to comfort His children, removing all trace of sorrow. How much closer could we come to God?

Reconciliation with others

In the end, we will also find perfect reconciliation with each other. This has been an ongoing struggle since the moment Adam blamed Eve. The church represents the greatest demonstration of inter-personal reconciliation the world has ever seen, although we haven't always lived up to our potential.

These final chapters reveal a people at peace with each other. In Revelation 21:9, an angel offers to show John "the bride, the wife of the Lamb," that is, the church as she will be when God's plan is finally in place. What John sees is a city, shining with God's glory.

This city is a perfect cube, "as wide and high as it is long" (Revelation 21:16). Whatever else this means, we can agree this city is perfectly proportioned and symmetrical, a picture of harmony among God's people, the church.

The angel shows John the splendid city wall. Its twelve gates are marked with the names of the twelve tribes of Israel and its foundations with the names of the twelve apostles. In this combination we're reminded how, through the gospel (represented by the apostles), God fulfills what He started among the Jews (represented by the twelve tribes). The struggle between Jew and Gentile that marred the church's witness is ended forever. Harmony reigns.

The twelve gates remain open, night and day (see Revelation 21:25), indicating an atmosphere of safety and security; "nothing impure will ever enter" this city, "nor will anyone who does what is shameful or deceitful, but only those whose names are written in the Lamb's book of life" (Revelation 21:27).

Like those in the Old Testament who sat securely beneath their own vine and fig tree (see Zechariah 3:10), residents of this city will have no need to fear others. The harmony promised in the New Jerusalem will never end. The nations will live together in peace and earth's rulers will come willingly to the city (see Revelation 21:24). Even the leaves from the trees are for the "healing of the nations" (Revelation 22:2).

Reconciliation with self

When God's plan is fully in place, each believer will be at peace with himself or herself. We see the most powerful evidence of this in Revelation 22:4: "They will see his face, and his name will be on their foreheads."

Remember the first sign of intra-personal alienation in the Garden? It was when Adam and Eve realized they were naked and hid from God's approach. They were ashamed of themselves and sought to avoid God's gaze.

How different the scene in the New Jerusalem! We look with confidence into God's face; all fear and shame are gone. God's "name will be on their foreheads" (Revelation 22:4b), our identity gloriously settled forever for we are marked as His own.

Reconciliation with nature

Under the curse humanity had lost any harmony with the natural world. In the "old order of things," labor was laborious, for both men and women. But what was lost in the first Garden is regained in the last.

Although described as a city, the New Jerusalem looks more like a park. "The river of the water of life" (Revelation 22:1-2) flows down the middle of the main street, with trees of life on each side. No longer off limits (see Genesis 3:22-24), anyone, anytime can eat the fruit from the tree of life.

Instead of nature being a hostile environment, now all creation is an ally, with plenty of water and food (see Revelation 21:6; 22:1-2), no more darkness (see Revelation 21:23, 25; 22:5), no threat of chaos as represented by the sea (see Revelation 21:1), no danger of death, no more reasons to mourn or cry, and no more pain (see Revelation 21:4).

Work was never part of the curse but in the "old order of things," it was difficult to see how our labor fulfilled God's mission in the world. Now that the curse is gone, so too is any confusion. Eternity is not idleness, it is delightful diligence, loved labor, work as worship.

In the New Jerusalem, we will be servants (see Revelation 22:3) and "reign for ever and ever" (Revelation 22:5). What a perfect description of what it means to finally and forever find your calling. You and I will live in the new heaven and new earth (Revelation 21:1) as rulers, having gained mastery of this new creation, just as God intended at the beginning (see Genesis 1:28). Our work will be done consciously and willingly as an act of service to God.

Consummation!

We have reached the consummation of God's plan and what a glorious picture it presents! All our broken relationships are restored, especially our relationship with Him.

At the center of this book is the One who is at the center of God's redemptive plan, Jesus. The sinless Son of God lived a life of obedience, even to the point of dying on the cross as the final sacrificial Lamb. God raised Him from the dead and pronounced

Him King of kings. He has the authority to bring to pass the final stage of God's plan until it shines in the New Jerusalem.

Seeing the big picture has allowed us to trace God's plan for reconciliation. We have moved through the Old Testament from the opening harmony, to alienation and resulting violence, to the beginning of God's plan with Abraham and Sarah. We have seen how God developed the nation of Israel and prepared it for the coming of Jesus.

The New Testament has revealed the person and work of Jesus, the key to God's plan, the picture that makes it all make sense. We have seen the gospel expanded and explained, then watched as it blossoms into consummation. The Bible is the story of reconciliation.

Knowing this is an important step forward in understanding the Bible. But knowing is not enough. God did not put this plan into effect only so we could understand it. He wants to be reconciled to you. He wants you to experience increasing harmony in your relationships with others and with yourself. He wants you to discover your calling and learn to cooperate with Him in your life work.

There is a place for you in God's plan. I invite you to experience the fullness of this plan in your life.

Study Questions

1. What other passages in the Book of Revelation speak of Jesus as the fulfillment of God's plan; as King; as unfolder of history?

2. Reflect on what it means to you that Jesus has fulfilled God's plan; that Jesus is supreme ruler over all earthly authorities; and that Jesus is the One who is able to unfold history.

3. What other passages can you find in the Book of Revelation that describe reconciliation with God, others, self, and nature?

4. What can you do to allow this plan of reconciliation to be more fully realized within you?

Scripture Index

Subject Index

Made in the USA
Middletown, DE
05 June 2019